Something Extra

Jill Roegge

ISBN 978-1-64569-013-9 (paperback)
ISBN 978-1-64569-014-6 (digital)

Copyright © 2019 by Jill Roegge

All rights reserved. No part of this publication may be reproduced, distributed, or transmitted in any form or by any means, including photocopying, recording, or other electronic or mechanical methods without the prior written permission of the publisher. For permission requests, solicit the publisher via the address below.

Christian Faith Publishing, Inc.
832 Park Avenue
Meadville, PA 16335
www.christianfaithpublishing.com

Printed in the United States of America

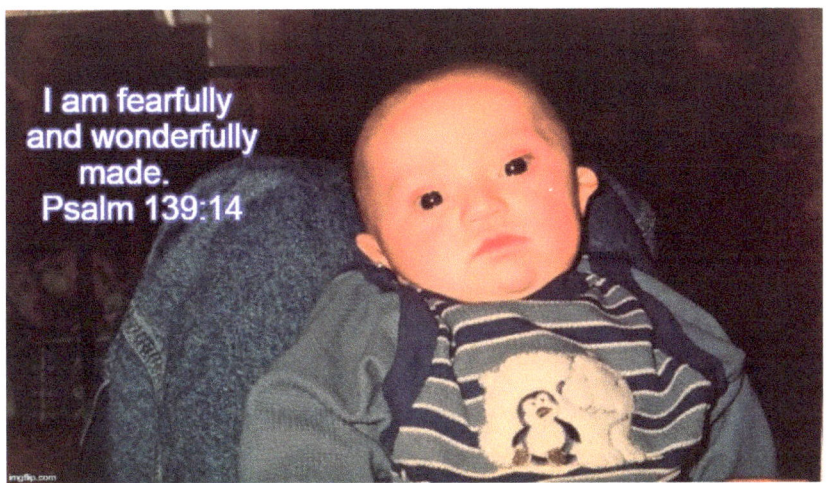

For Isaac

1

When Isaac began kindergarten at our local public school, he was really one of the first students to be educated "in-house" who had a significant diagnosis. Our little school was taking a leap by allowing Isaac to attend school. Our town, population nearly four hundred, was already "watching" Isaac.

Now, I was sending him to school and opening ourselves up for scrutinizing by an entire school filled with "normal" kids! It was a huge adjustment for the teachers. Isaac was going to be in a regular education class with a full time 1:1 aide. None of these teachers had ever had a student like Isaac in their classrooms, and it was difficult for them. I think it was a great learning experience for them. No, they had not signed up to be a special education teacher, but life sometimes hands us the unexpected, even in a classroom.

Usually at the beginning of the school year, the teachers were very nervous—understandably—didn't know what to expect, and perhaps somewhat irritated that they were going to have such a situation in their room. Everyone survived. And by the end of the first quarter, teachers were beginning to understand him.

By the end of the second quarter, the teachers had relaxed quite a bit and were actually smiling at parent-teacher conferences. By the end of the third quarter, most teachers felt that they had a great handle on Isaac. And most times, at the end of the fourth quarter, the teachers had bonded so well with Isaac. They were actually going to miss him!

What about his classmates? A great worry of mine was always how Isaac would get along with his peers. Starting in kindergarten, there was a group of girls who sort of mothered over Isaac—in a good way. The boys were tolerant of Isaac and nice to him, but the girls protected him, helped him, and took him under their wings.

I'm sure Isaac was annoying in elementary school. I know he easily got on kids' nerves, made inappropriate noises, and in general, was just an oddity to his peers.

In early elementary school, it was difficult to understand why someone was different and why they behave differently. It wasn't something easily comprehended by little kids.

Then, as Isaac aged, I felt as though he became more separated from the boys his age. He didn't have anything in common with them, and it became more awkward for them to relate to him. But those sweet girls still looked out for him and really put up with him!

By the time Isaac entered high school, the maturity of his peers was now at a level where they could understand him. They could feel comfortable engaging him in conversations, playing along with his silliness, and help correct him when he was doing something socially inappropriate. He was accepted. And those sweet girls continued to watch over him!

Isaac is a senior this year. The last two years his classmates have really shown their acceptance of Isaac and tried to include him at ball games, activities, dances, etc. He had even been invited to go out to eat supper by a friend, been asked to prom, and this fall, he was voted homecoming king by his peers!

To me, this speaks volumes about the selflessness of his peers. They were willing to give up a social honor and give it to Isaac—to let him be honored. Isaac was very pleased, but I actually think these kids were so happy FOR Isaac. They wanted HIM to be happy! And he was! What an amazing group of kids!

This event will always make my heart smile. These kids have been with Isaac since kindergarten. These twenty-two to twenty-five kids have given him acceptance, love, fun, and friendship, and I couldn't be more pleased that he has grown up with these compassionate classmates!

SOMETHING EXTRA

Isaac and his friends from Triopia High School

2

WARNING: I wrote this during a *dark* time, so I apologize for my negativity!

Just because we have a family member who has Down syndrome does not mean things are always "warm and fuzzy" in our home. As I typed this, I'd just shed a few tears, and my blood pressure was no doubt much higher than it should be. Nothing major, just typical daily "stuff."

Isaac has been shouting at me at the top of his lungs (I think our windows were vibrating) because I was telling him he needed to turn his iPad music down.

He was yelling no, and I gave him the option of going to his room and listen to his iPad there, or staying in the living room using headphones, both of which seemed like end-of-the-world solutions to Isaac, so he chose yelling at me instead. Not just yelling but interspersing whistling between the screams.

Usually whistling is a happy thing but when used as a rebellious tactic, whistling is not happy. Isaac knows he is only to whistle OUTSIDE, so he is adding fuel to his argument by whistling and yelling.

Prior to his yelling, Isaac was going room to room and shutting off all the lights because that is how he likes to view lightning. But when other people are needing to see, it is a true annoyance to have someone repeatedly turning the lights off and arguing ensues between the brothers. And right before he was turning the lights out, he was attempting to use the restroom by himself and things got messy.

It really was okay that I shared this information to the worldwide web because it will all be told tomorrow to everyone who Isaac will see. His side of the story will include some of these: Jill mad.

Jill very angry. Music too loud. Isaac yelled. Jill not like yelling. Isaac not like headphones. No whistling inside. Charlie mad, lights off.

He will tell everyone he sees about the experience because he always tells on himself and waits for them to acknowledge and reinforce that he needs to do what Jill says.

Is this a reason I should be tearful and upset? Probably not. But when it happens day after day and I look back at how long I've been doing this and that I don't feel we ever make progress, it is frustrating. It is maddening. It hits me hard. And guess what? Things aren't going to change.

This is our life. Cynical? Yes. Yes I am. And I also just had a bad evening so my cynicism was shining. I see people my age who are sitting back, relaxing, and enjoying life. I see people who parent their kids part-time, people who have all sorts of time to themselves to have a hobby—a vacation, a date night.

I see people who couldn't survive a week in our household because it would be too much work for them. They have no idea what it takes to parent someone who needs extra help. They don't get it. This isn't the most uplifting news, but the truth is, there are some frustrating days. Not everyone who has a child with Down syndrome will have these days, but Isaac is eighteen (almost nineteen—fifty-six days till his birthday).

He has an IQ of about forty. He is like a four-year-old trapped in an adult's body, so we have these days. So I put him to bed, tuck him in, kiss him, and he says, "Mommyyy," and I know that he does love me. He's frustrated too. And I think he knows that it is always going to be him and me. We spend so much time together that it is easy for him to take his frustrations out on me. Tomorrow will be a new day.

Isaac with his siblings: Aaron, Lydia & Charlie

3

When Isaac was born, his older brother, Aaron "Buck," was a freshman in high school. Being a freshman in and of itself is rather an awkward time, but then add to it that you're getting a baby brother. And oh, by the way, the baby is going to have Down syndrome. That's a lot to deal with as a teenager.

Isaac only refers to him as "Buck," so if you ask him about "Aaron," he won't have a clue who you are talking about!

I remember our family having conversations about Down syndrome before Isaac was born and one of Buck's ideas was getting a dog because he had read that people with disabilities often respond well to animals and enjoy the companionship of a dog! (There may have been an ulterior motive here on his part, but nonetheless, it was sweet of him to be thinking about Isaac's welfare!)

Isaac loves to be around Buck. Buck has two dogs and Isaac always wants to know what he is doing and where his dogs are! Apparently, Buck was right about the dog idea! I know throughout the years there have been times when Isaac has done embarrassing behaviors or acted inappropriately when we were at Buck's high school activities, but never did Buck roll his eyes, back away in embarrassment, or detach himself from Isaac. Buck has always been very compassionate with Isaac and understanding of the attention required to care for Isaac.

Isaac's arrival into the family mix was an adjustment for everyone, but each family member accepted him and rallied to support him. I've always felt I somewhat let Buck and Lydia down by giving them a brother who wasn't "perfect." They haven't made me feel that way. It is just my feelings. You always want to give your kids the best of everything, and I remember having to deliver the news of the diagnosis to them and feeling like I was really disappointing them. I was giving them a brother who was really going to change their world, and although he wasn't a "perfect" baby brother, he has fit perfectly into their lives, and I couldn't be happier or more proud of the relationships that Isaac has with his siblings Buck, Lydia, and Charlie!

Isaac with his siblings: Lydia, Isaac, Charlie and Aaron

4

The brotherly relationship between Isaac and Charlie fluctuates between amazing and "rocky"! Isaac was twelve when Charlie was born. The first couple of years didn't really have any noticeable effect on Charlie one way or another. He was a baby who was getting used to his surroundings and the people who spent the most time with him.

Isaac has always LOVED babies, so of course, he was thrilled with Charlie! As Charlie has aged, he has asked questions: Why is Isaac acting like this? When will Isaac be done with Down syndrome? Why can't Isaac do _____?

Again, we have explained as much about Down syndrome as we can to Charlie. I know it is frustrating to Charlie. Isaac is not a typical older brother. There are so many things he can't do. Charlie's maturity level has surpassed Isaac's. Isaac is the size of a man but doesn't act like a man. I asked Charlie how he felt about being Isaac's brother, and these are his words:

"I like that Isaac says math problems and does flash cards because I sometimes have them at school and then I know the answer! I like Isaac's hugs even though they are tight sometimes. It's fine with me that he has Down syndrome. It's frustrating that we don't always understand him. I get tired of his routines—listening to the same songs over and over and always having to eat at McDonald's.

"It's embarrassing that he tells everyone what goes on at our house—all our secrets (who was mad, who had gas, who was picking their nose). Will Isaac get married? I don't want him to move out even though we argue. It would be fun to have an older brother who was normal. Maybe somebody like Buck, someone who could play ball with me, take me on rides, hang out, go to ballgames, play with my toys with me. It's hard to not get mad at him sometimes."

They love each other. They are typical siblings who try and boss each other around, tease each other, argue, and laugh. Do not let Isaac fool you. He is an instigator in picking little fights with Charlie! There are often times when the role reversal is obvious.

I've seen Charlie reach for Isaac's hand in public, not because Charlie needs it but because Charlie knows he needs to help Isaac. I've seen Charlie help tie Isaac's shoes. Charlie patiently comforts Isaac when he is upset. I know it is very difficult for him to have to be patient with someone who is so much older than he is. It should be the other way around. I feel that as Charlie continues to age and mature, he will develop more of an understanding of "how Isaac is," and he will have even more compassion. I have to remind myself he is just seven. He's still learning—just like the rest of us!

Isaac and Charlie

SOMETHING EXTRA

Isaac and Charlie

5

My daughter, Lydia, was in kindergarten when Isaac was born. We had prepared her with as much information about Down syndrome that we thought a five-year-old could comprehend. She was mostly just excited about having a baby brother but also wondered if it meant we could get a handicapped license plate! Sorry, no.

Lydia has wholeheartedly embraced Isaac since day one. She took an interest in watching the therapists who began coming to our house to work with Isaac (beginning when he was six weeks old). She heard and absorbed all of the conversations about his health, his development, his needs, his strengths and weaknesses. Having a younger sibling with different circumstances forced Lydia into maturity at a faster pace.

She was often "overlooked" and took a back seat when it came to garnering my attention. Sometimes it couldn't have been helped. Isaac simply required more time, more attention, and more help. Looking back, I never detected even a hint of jealousy of the attention Isaac received. She wanted to be helpful to me and also Isaac.

As the older sister, she became a champion advocate and protector of Isaac. She helped with his care so I could do cooking and household chores. She creatively engaged him with activities. Her patience with Isaac NEVER wavered (mine often did). When I would become frustrated with Isaac, she would sense it and "take over" and give me the break I needed. She became that kid who corrected people who used the word "retard."

Out of love and respect for her little brother, she did many things on her own, knowing that I needed to be assisting Isaac. She knew I was overwhelmed with Isaac, and I never recall her asking anything of me. She handled things for herself so as not to bother me.

SOMETHING EXTRA

Did I ever feel guilty about this discrepancy of attention? You bet, I did! I still do! The selflessness and compassion that Lydia possesses is beyond comparison to any I have ever witnessed. I would imagine that many siblings in Lydia's situation could have rebelled, turned away, expressed jealousy, and left the house as soon as she could. Not Lydia. Her relationship with Isaac brought her home most weekends of college because she missed her brothers! Her career as an occupational therapist is a direct result of Isaac.

The bond between Lydia and Isaac is like no other. Sometimes, I'm actually a bit envious of their closeness. Isaac always says "maaa" to Lydia, and we've deduced that is his way of saying "I love you." They say it back-and-forth to each other. He doesn't say it to anyone else, and he doesn't want anyone else to say it to him except Lydia. It is reserved solely for her! It should come as no surprise that Lydia chose Isaac to be her man of honor at her wedding—a role he performed perfectly. She has never been embarrassed of Isaac and has always been protective. The sibling role is a difficult one, but boy, did Isaac get blessed with an incredible sister!

Isaac and Lydia: the day Isaac was born; the day Lydia got married

Some of the loved ones he's lost, and the photos he cherishes.

6

Isaac has been profoundly affected by losses of loved ones, and he has unique ways of dealing with it. My dad passed away when Isaac was eight, and Isaac surprised us all by not really showing much sadness at that time.

Isaac had been very present during my dad's illness and hospice care, so he witnessed the decline and seemed to accept that Grampa was gone and didn't ask any questions. He just "knew" everything was okay, and he was in heaven.

However, about six months later, he began crying about it. It just took him longer to process it—a delayed reaction. He talks about Grampa a lot and has a picture of them together that he carries around the house and talks to (personally, I think they do converse). He occasionally has tearful moments while talking to his picture of Grampa.

Several times a week, he brings me the music "It Is Well With My Soul" so I will play it on the piano for him. This song was played at my dad's funeral, and Isaac loves to sing it. Usually, after I have played it, he feels better, as if he was brought closer to him when it was played.

When Matt's parents passed away, Isaac was a teenager, circumstances were different, and he didn't have an opportunity for good-byes or closure. I thought that him being older would perhaps make it easier on Isaac. Not the case. Isaac has been "stuck" in grief. He has a picture of Matt's mom that goes from room to room with him in our house. He talks to her. He plays "How Great Thou Art" sometimes twenty-plus times per day, as that song was at Dave and Judy's funerals.

He has major meltdowns often, which we have curbed somewhat by making the rule that if he is going to weep because of his music, he will have to take it into his room.

Isaac seems to seek approval and opinions from Judy also. He talks to her picture and asks her questions and again, I wouldn't be at all surprised if they were communicating. Almost on a daily basis, he says "miss her" or "love her," and we reassure him that she loved him!

Last night, Charlie had a ballgame at Trinity, where Judy taught for so many years. Isaac had a meltdown with major tears when we mentioned we were going to the game. He has done this at the mention of other games at Trinity. He cried and said "miss her!"

We finally pieced it together that he associates Judy so much with Trinity that it is too difficult for him to be there, and we aren't going to push it.

I know there are people who do not believe Isaac to be capable of deep emotions. I know there are people who wouldn't believe Isaac is capable of understanding loss. I know he has Down syndrome. Who would think his emotions matter? Well, let me tell you, Isaac has a true heart capable of such deep love and compassion. Those of us who are "normal" try and keep our grief on a timeline and don't always express our emotions as fully as we would like—we are inhibited. He is real. Those who he has loved have left a deep imprint on his heart, and the reunion they shall have one day will be beyond joyous!

SOMETHING EXTRA

Isaac with 2 Gramma Judys and sister Lydia

Isaac with Papa Wayne

7

I've provided some insight into Isaac's skills, personal care needs, and behaviors. Our family is accustomed to these needs and daily challenges. Now, we send Isaac to school and guess what? Someone has to deal with all of it there!

Isaac has been BEYOND blessed with the 1:1 aides/paraprofessionals and special education teachers he has had over the years. These people spend seven hours a day, five days a week with Isaac. They have all learned how to "read" Isaac and understand him. This isn't easy. It doesn't happen overnight, and it takes a ton of patience!

When Isaac gets to school, the aide has to take over as parent, try and keep him behaving, try to help him learn, modify assignments, redirect him so often, help with toileting, help him change into PE clothes, be his "interpreter," be his advocate, discipline him when needed, and try and keep him in a good mood, which can be a challenge depending on so many factors (events that happened at home, weather, and things that happen/change at school).

Folks, NEVER underestimate the value of competent special education staff and paraprofessionals! So much is expected from these people, yet their value is never fully appreciated. In our experience, the people who have worked with Isaac have become like other parents to him, and they, in return, have truly embraced Isaac and developed a mutual level of affection.

SOMETHING EXTRA

Paraprofessionals and teachers who have worked with Isaac over the years.

8

We provide constant supervision over Isaac at home. He isn't to be trusted on his own. There are things he would get in to, there is food he would eat, and there are safety concerns. For instance, he knows scissors will cut his hair (he's done it) but doesn't realize they could cut him. He may get hungry and try to fix eggs (a favorite) but wouldn't realize leaving the gas on could create a fire. If he were to get thirsty and try to pour a drink, there would be a huge mess. He requires supervision for his own protection. I try not to hover, but at the same time, I must be diligent and keep him protected as he is so naive.

We live in the country, so there isn't much of a risk of him getting in traffic. However, when we go to a store's parking lot, he has absolutely no understanding that cars could hit him. He doesn't watch for cars. It doesn't even enter his mind. I have "trained" him to always wait in the car until I open his door: first, so he doesn't exit into traffic, and second, to prevent him from dinging someone's door. And whenever I open his door, he's waiting for me, he gets out, and he automatically takes my hand so we can walk through the parking lot.

There are times I tell him that he doesn't need to hold my hand since we are walking side by side, but he still reaches for my hand, and I'm happy with that. I remember attending a convention for parents of kids with disabilities about seventeen years ago. I recall seeing women in their sixties and seventies who were walking around holding their adult children's hands, shuffling along together. I remember wondering if that would be me, and I have become THAT mom!

I look back at those older ladies and think of the lifetime of care and supervision they provided, how tired they must be, do they have regrets, how full their hearts must be, how much they gave up to continually provide care and supervision to their child, how their lives could have been different, wondering what will happen to that child when the shuffling parent is gone. I will continue supervising him at home, holding his hand, pouring his drinks, plugging in his iPad, and I will continue to be blessed.

Jill and Isaac

9

Isaac is limited in his self-care skills. He is rather "low functioning" in his motor skills. I am the first to admit that I am probably a big part of this learned helplessness. But my intentions were good! I have always known that people give Isaac an extra glance, and sometimes, it is more than a glance, due solely to his physical appearance. I often notice people staring a bit, probably just out of curiosity, and that's fine with me (most of the time). However, I have never wanted to give people any other reason to stare or judge him, so I have usually done most of his grooming/personal hygiene. I want it done right. I want him to be clean and acceptable.

Could he do some of these tasks? Probably. He is very limited in his fine motor skills, so he truly does have difficulty brushing his teeth, washing himself, dressing, etc. And we are usually always in a hurry in the mornings, so it is just easier for me to do it.

My long-range plan is to improve his self-care skills once we don't have the morning racing getting ready for school. In the meantime, our family does it all: brush his teeth, shower him, dry him, wipe him, dress him, shave him, etc. I know I have brought this burden on myself, and there are many days when I'm bathing him that I actually have to say to myself, "When you do this for the least of my brethren, you are doing it for me." It then becomes easier for me to finish the task with a more positive attitude.

I know in his own way that Isaac "appreciates" me, but after nearly nineteen years of the daily care, there are days it wears us down. Although I'm thankful for the blessing of Isaac, there are moments when I must remind myself that I have been entrusted by God to take care of this precious being. God put him in MY life. He is a gift.

SOMETHING EXTRA

And just when I'm feeling frustrated by the daily care, Isaac gives me his famous smile, and I feel that God is smiling right back at me.

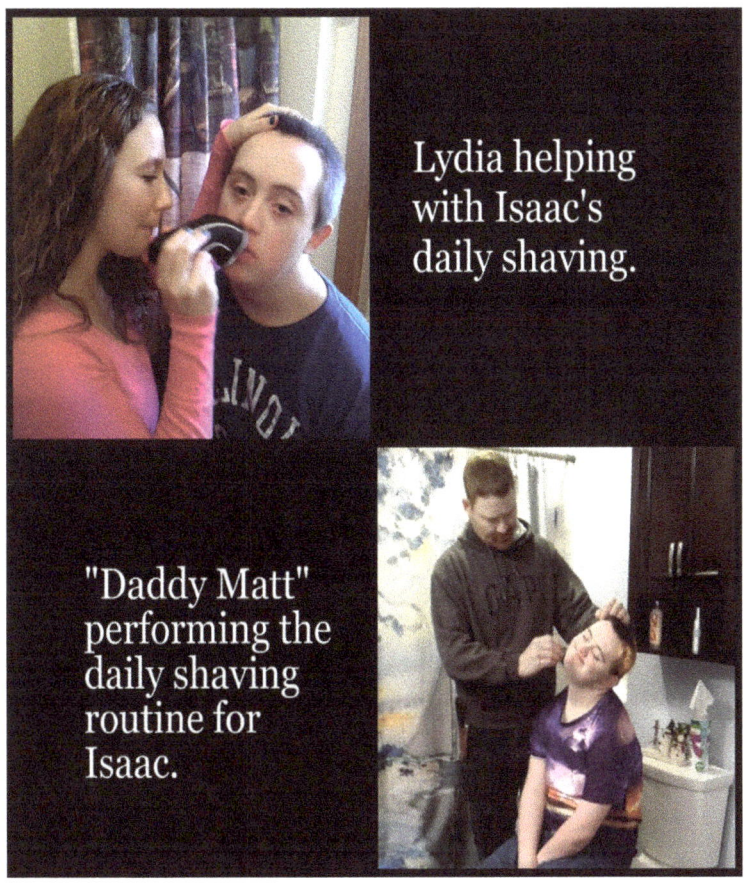

Lydia helping with Isaac's daily shaving.

"Daddy Matt" performing the daily shaving routine for Isaac.

10

The general population has this theory about people with Down syndrome: they are always happy. I'm sorry to shatter people's beliefs here, but that is definitely not true in Isaac's case! Typically, he is a happy, carefree guy. But he experiences an entire range of emotions just like anyone else. I can give you a very recent example (unfortunately!).

There was no school yesterday, so Isaac spent his day with me at my office. Good day, everything went well. After work, we stopped by at Lydia and Wade's house, and he somehow thought he was spending the night there and when we left, he was a little grumpy and didn't quite understand why he was leaving because he thought he would stay there. So it was a tense ride home for him. He was disappointed. Okay, he was upset. I tried to brighten his mood by discussing supper!

Earlier in the day, Matt had suggested we go out for supper, something Isaac thoroughly enjoys. Communication skills aren't always practiced in a high form in our household, and somewhere along the way, Matt and I had decided we would just eat at home. Change of plans + Isaac = very emotionally difficult times. Isaac became loud.

We asked him to join us in the kitchen; he refused. He stayed in his spot in the living room protesting by shaking his head. He did some yelling. We tried the singsong tone of voice approach to encourage him to come eat. No luck. We tried a more stern approach. He wouldn't budge. This guy loves to eat, but because it wasn't the situation he expected, he was unable to change. It is very frustrating to try and remain calm when it is so simple to me: come in and eat, we will go out another time. No. That is beyond him. He refused every attempt we made to get him to join us.

We ate without him. He kept glaring at us and shaking his head. We cleaned up the kitchen and rejoined him, but he wouldn't engage with us in any way. This scenario stresses all of us and really kicks the fun/joy out of everyone's moods. An hour and a half later, he said he was ready to eat. Part of me wanted to say, "too late, you missed your chance," but I also realize that change and the unexpected is so difficult for him, and it often literally takes him an hour or longer to process what is/isn't happening. Some may feel I'm babying him by letting him eat when he was ready, but things often have to be on HIS time, when he is ready and not until then. Our household was in high stress mode from 5:45 p.m. to 8:45 p.m. because we decided not to go out to eat. Felt like an entirely wasted evening. People with Down syndrome are happy all the time? No, they are human like the rest of us!

Isaac being upset, mad, and lying down to protest.

11

Isaac doesn't have many hobbies really. His favorite activities at home are using his iPad and occasionally shooting baskets. When he gets home from school, he goes to his spot on the love seat to "relax." He always sits in the same place and never wants anyone next to him (unless it is time for bed, and he wants to snuggle… with Matt!).

This summer, we moved our furniture around to see if we could get him to try a new spot. He outsmarted us and sat on the floor in the exact spot where the love seat had been. After two months, we gave in and moved it back for him.

What does he do on the iPad? He listens to music, watches old episodes of *Mr. Rogers*, *Teletubbies*, *The Wiggles*, and *Sesame Street*. He has a fireworks app that he enjoys and a rain/thunderstorm app that brings him great joy! He has a couple of bingo apps that he also plays. He LOVES listening to Joey and Rory singing "How Great Thou Art" and plays it dozens of times a day.

Many times he gets very emotional during the song (as it was played at David and Judy's funerals), so we have a rule that if he is going to become sad/tearful, he will need to play a different song or he can go in his room and listen to it. We aren't trying to be mean to him or discourage him from expressing his emotions, but he becomes "stuck" in his sadness, and it affects others in the house. He doesn't watch TV, with the exception of *America's Funniest Home Videos*. His simplistic hobbies and lifestyle bring him great happiness. What more could a guy want?

SOMETHING EXTRA

12

Often with Down syndrome there is a dual diagnosis—Down syndrome + Attention Deficit Disorder, Down syndrome + Obsessive Compulsive Disorder, Down syndrome + autism. Isaac falls into this category as he has Down syndrome, ADD, OCD, and is also on the autism spectrum! There are several mannerisms/idiosyncrasies that Isaac exhibits because of these diagnoses. For instance, Isaac LOVES numbers! He has such a fascinating relationship with them. Some of his favorite things include calculators, bingo cards, people's ages, road signs, and weather stats. I can't help but wonder how his brain reacts when he sees numbers. He is delighted when he sees numbers that he has a connection to. It may almost be like fireworks going off in his mind! Numbers truly mean something to him. He associates numbers with people; it can be a person's age or an athlete's jersey number. If he knows your age, he will not forget it, and he will automatically advance you on your next birthday without missing a beat. He plays Bingo a couple of times a month, and I feel he looks at the bingo card and somehow sees the numbers representing people he knows. When he hears the numbers announced, he shouts their names. Here are some examples: B–2 Jansen Joehl (football number about five years ago), B–3 Everett (his cousin who is three), B–7 Charlie Roegge (he's seven) B–9 John Love (football number many years ago) B–10 Isaac Werries (football number last year), I–20 Isaac, I–26 Lydia, G–55 Aunt Sue.

You get the idea by now. He also has committed to his memory the ages of people he knows who have passed away. For instance, O–71 is "Papa Wayne, Good Guy", O–67 is "Judy Roegge, Good Lady", O–73 is Uncle Charlie, O–68 is David Roegge, O–75 is Allen Beard.

SOMETHING EXTRA

These connections aren't just recalled on the Bingo card. We can drive down a road and see a speed limit sign and he will call out their names. Speed limit 55 "Gannon Greene" (former football player). Route 67 "Judy Roegge, Good Lady". He calls out people's names when he sees the temperature on his digital weather station. It is endless. He sees numbers everywhere and I often wonder how it is displayed in his mind.

It makes Isaac truly happy to be punching numbers on a calculator and showing me the numbers and saying the name of the corresponding person. It was also recently discovered that Isaac knows his multiplication facts! I'm certain he just has them memorized but it is pretty cool! If you hold up a multiplication flash card to him, he will tell you the correct answer! This comes from his repetitious hobby of using a calculator and flash cards.

If Isaac is calculating his flash cards and an answer is one of his connections, he is thrilled and makes an announcement and holds up the card. Cousin Arthur is zero (he's an infant); Matt is 41, Jill is 49. The numbers that must be swirling around in his head almost make me dizzy! While watching the nightly weather, he associates a name with each temperature or weather factor that is displayed: 68 degrees in Champaign- David Roegge; 25 mph winds-Lydia (La-La); High of 75 tomorrow-Allen Beard; Low of 41 tonight-Tara Hobrock.

When Matt gets home from farming and enters the back door, Isaac frequently announces, "41!!" And Matt returns with "19!!"

Last Friday night at Triopia's football game, Isaac was being his typical social self and then began talking about Grampa Wayne and Gramma Judy (who were not in attendance at the game!). He kept saying their names, and I was just replying with mundane responses, until Isaac pointed. Yep, there on the sidelines was Grampa Wayne (71) and Gramma Judy (80), standing side by side. His mind amazes me.

JILL ROEGGE

13

To go along with Isaac's love of numbers, I must also mention his love of counting! He possesses a unique blend of OCD and autism when it comes to counting. He is obsessed with counting, and often, there is a specific repetitive pattern. As an example: EVERY day, he counts in the shower. He counts the number of cups of water he pours over his head. He does a lot of self-talk. After he is clean, I let him have some water time in the shower, and I often hear him talking to himself, "Ten cups. Okay. Ten cups? Yes. Ten cups." And he proceeds counting cups of water and pouring them over his head.

It often ends up being many more than ten, as I get busy doing something else. Then as he exits the shower, he must step on his towel eleven times. Always eleven. When brushing his teeth (to which I am scripted to daily sing "Hallelu, Hallelu!"), he rinses his mouth five times. Don't try and get away with three or four. It must be five.

Counting is part of his ritual. We listen to the "Chicken Dance" four times on the way to school. If we drive to Jacksonville, we can hear it a total of nine times. If I try to turn it off before the ninth time, I'm reminded we were only on the seventh or eighth time. MUST BE NINE! He is able to mentally keep track of how many times he listens to a song, and that is amazing because he may listen to a song fifteen times in a row.

Those are just a few examples of how counting fits into his routine. He has added yet another way to incorporate counting into his daily life recently—counting items. And by items, I mean just about anything: cars, cows, suns, moons, stars, eggs, trees, daddies, poops, tractors, noses, cokes, Debbies (a favorite name), deer, shirts, lights, toes. He isn't counting the number of these items he sees, he is just counting for fun. "1 Debbie, 2 Debbies, 3 Debbies, 4 Debbies, 100 Debbies, etc.!"

I have been encouraging him to only count up to ten of any item because honestly, when he gets to the sixty-seventh Debbie (or any other item), I'm fairly weary of the counting. If you have a conversation with Isaac, he may tell you "stop counting ____(fill in the blank)____" and that just means I've told him, "let's stop counting_____." Counting is a wonderful skill, and he loves his numbers!

Two Isaacs:
Isaac French
Isaac Werries

14

During my pregnancy with Isaac, our prayer had been please let him be healthy! And he was! He does have a few medical issues that are associated with Down syndrome, but he has been remarkably healthy in his near nineteen years.

There are several interesting things about Isaac, one being his response to pain. I know he feels pain, but it is a rather delayed response, and perhaps he doesn't have the ability to determine the locale of his pain. Several instances in his lifetime were when he had some fairly significant injuries: a fractured finger, a hand closed in a door, boiling hot grease down his bare back (instant blisters), and he hasn't acknowledged he was in pain.

Many routine trips to a doctor have ended with it being discovered he had nasty ear infections. If Isaac DOES complain of pain, it MUST be severe. We usually have to assess him from head to foot and use process of elimination to figure out where he's hurting. I may look in his mouth and see a terribly red, sore-looking throat, and if I ask him if it hurts, he may say no. He may instead say neck hurts or head hurts. He can't pinpoint his pain.

When he finally realizes he is in pain, the reaction is often quite dramatic. He cries. Loudly and mournfully. Early this year, during a hospital stay, hospital staff continually asked him to rate his pain. Isaac loves numbers but also has no clue what a "ten scale" is. He'd say a random number and then the staff would look at me and ask, "You think about an eight or so?"

How do I know? I have learned over the years that certain behaviors he exhibits are related to how he is feeling. If he says he's not hungry, it typically indicates he has a sore throat. If he doesn't finish his plate of food, it most likely means he has a stomach ache. We have to watch Isaac's behavior for cues that he may not be feeling well. Pain is often a guessing game with Isaac.

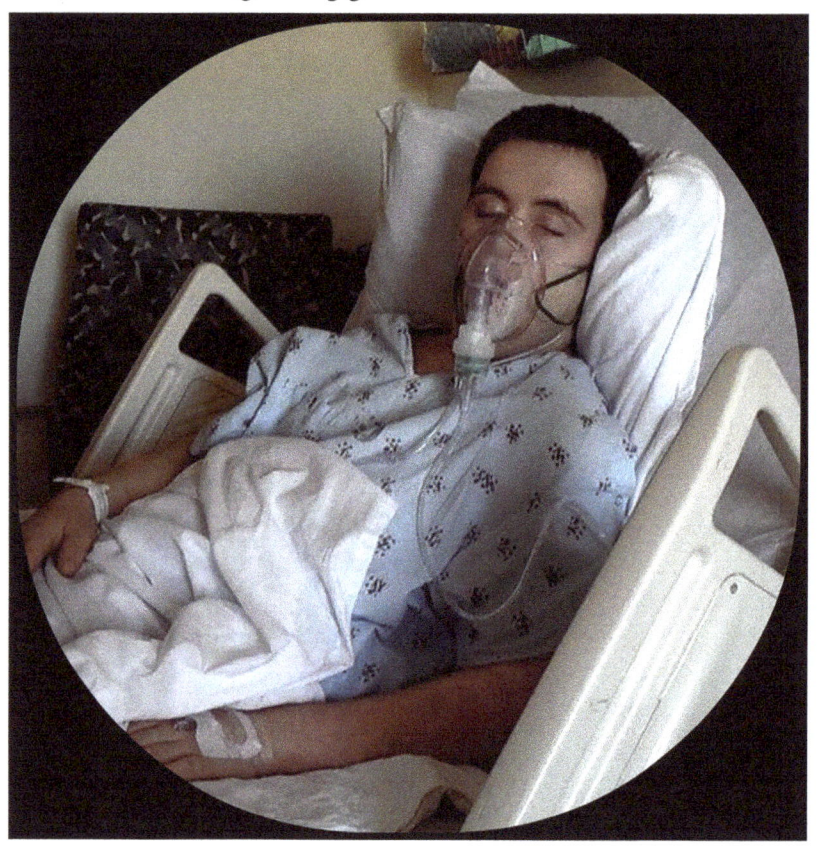

15

Everyone reacts in their own way when given unexpected news. I don't believe there is a right/wrong way. It is an individual response. I've never been particularly good at showing raw emotion. I prefer to muster up strength and put on the best positive face I can.

The news that Isaac was going to have Down syndrome came to me at about 6:30 one summer evening during supper. My ob-gyn phoned me and asked if I was home alone. Nope, the family is all here eating supper. Buck (fourteen at the time) and Lydia (five) were clanking their dishes and silverware so I excused myself to the back porch.

Dr. Saint said he had the results of my amniocentesis. My baby has Down syndrome. He needed to tell me that I had options: I could terminate, I could put the baby up for adoption, or I could keep it.

My response was I was having and keeping the baby, to which he replied, "You have just made my job a lot easier." He went on to ask if I wanted to know the gender.

"Yes, give me something else to think about."

He said, "It's a boy!" He told me things were going to be okay, and he would give me as much guidance and information as he could. And he did.

Shortly after the phone call, my sister Sally came down the street to visit, and my mom and dad came over. We all talked about this news that was going to change our family. There were many tears. I wanted to make sure everyone was okay with this. Those two kids at the supper table weren't sure what was going on, and I probably didn't do a very good job of talking to them that night. I didn't have a clue what to tell them. I was sad. I was very scared. I didn't know anything about Down syndrome. How was this baby going to affect our family? Was he going to be healthy? I'd never been around anyone who had it. What in the world was I going to do?

Isaac: 2 weeks old
Aaron: 14 years
Lydia: 5 years

16

Along with other awareness initiatives, October is Down Syndrome Awareness Month. Our family continues our advocacy efforts this month by providing a glimpse into how Down syndrome impacts our lives. Isaac has been and continues to be our teacher and tour guide on this adventure. We are still learning as we go!

Today, the lesson is this: as humans, we are woven together and typically have only "pairs" of chromosomes. Down syndrome (also called Trisomy 21) occurs when there is a third copy of the twenty-first chromosome caused by some error in cell division. Due to this extra genetic material, the typical course of development is altered and several characteristics may occur including low muscle tone, upwardly slanted eyes, short stature, a single deep crease across the palm of a hand, a slightly flattened facial profile, and several other identifying features.

Not everyone with Down syndrome has all of these characteristics, and they occur in varying degrees. A couple of characteristics we weren't warned about were silliness and stubbornness! The day I received the prenatal diagnosis for Isaac, that he would have Down syndrome, I sure didn't feel it was a good day. In fact, I felt it was a devastating day. Isaac's life has blessed me beyond my wildest expectations.

JILL ROEGGE

Isaac before going to prom!
Pictured with his sister, Lydia, and her husband, Wade

(Isaac refers to them as "La-La" and "Sparkle")

17

Current information from the National Down Syndrome Society indicates that 1 in every 691 babies born in the United States will have Down syndrome, which means approximately 6,000 babies are born with Down syndrome each year. Isaac was born in 1998 and within a year, another baby in Arenzville was born with Down syndrome. I don't believe our little town has had another incidence of Down syndrome since then!

Oftentimes in a rural area, it is difficult to find resources or other parents who are in a similar situation. Fortunately for our family, we became acquainted with some families who helped us "learn the ropes," answered many of our questions, and gave us reassurance that things would be okay. These parents have perhaps been the greatest resource we have found. I've always felt that parents of kids with special needs or a certain diagnosis are in a sort of club. Not that we "chose" membership, but it is a bond we share. And taking that further, I feel it is my responsibility to assist other parents or at least make an offer of assistance to new parents who are in a situation they didn't expect.

Not everyone wants help, and that is fine! I'm thankful for the guidance and advice given to me by some pretty amazing parents: Gail Olson, Leta Holtschlag, Laurie Crews, Jennifer Keaton, Cheryl Baer, and Laurie Buhlig. It really does "take a village" sometimes!

18

Isaac loves telling people he eats steak for supper. It gets a laugh. Truth is he doesn't eat steak. He would have great difficulty eating steak and pork. As he always says when people mention pork, "trouble with the pork!"

If you have ever noticed, Isaac has extremely tiny teeth. Several are baby teeth (with no permanent ones underneath), and the teeth he has are very ground down. He grinds/grits his teeth most nights and doesn't use them much for eating. Much of his eating consists of using his tongue and sort of mashing food on the roof of his mouth. He doesn't do much chewing! This is why he has trouble with pork or steak. He prefers foods that are soft—scrambled eggs, pudding, pasta, ground beef. He loves a hamburger but will bite into it and then use his tongue/roof of mouth. He is very aware of what foods he can easily eat. He makes his own food decisions and "allows" himself what he can handle. And we do still cut most of his food for him (more of that learned helplessness!) due to choking incidents. He knows which foods may cause him to choke and will refuse to eat them. He will stop himself from eating something if he is having trouble with it. So when he says he has steak for supper, the joke is on you!

SOMETHING EXTRA

19

We knew before Isaac was born that he would have Down syndrome. This gave us a head start. We could read, prepare, and try to be "ready" for this new situation. We were able to do paperwork and line up early intervention services for Isaac. Babies with Down syndrome will have developmental delays and will greatly benefit from EI services. In our case, this included physical, speech, developmental, and occupational therapies. These began in our home when Isaac was a month old. Each of these therapies helped Isaac with his basic physical, cognitive, language, and social skills. These therapists came to our home weekly, often two times per week, and worked with Isaac and helped our family understand how we could work with Isaac to encourage his development. This was a crucial part of Isaac's first three years of life. Invaluable services and influence by outstanding therapists who became such an important part of our family's life.

SOMETHING EXTRA

Isaac with his therapists (physical, speech, developmental and occupational), who would come to work with him each week in our home.

JILL ROEGGE

Isaac watching for clouds and rain.

20

It is somewhat ironic, I think, that Isaac brings so much "sunshine" to my life yet HIS favorite type of weather is cloudy, rainy days. He LOVES weather events! He is so tickled when it becomes windy. He has his face pressed up against his window if the sky is the least bit threatening-looking, hoping to see lightning!

Okay, actually I'd describe him as nearly obsessed with weather! He has a weather station by his "spot" in the living room, he annually receives a weather calendar as a Christmas gift, and he now has an official weather radio. He enjoys looking at the radar to see what could be coming. I believe he almost senses when it is going to rain, snow, or have a change in weather. I've always thought he somehow "felt" weather changes. Maybe it is the air pressure affecting him, who knows?

The other night we walked outside, it was dark, and Isaac said, "I smell rain!" Within a couple hours, we did have a small amount of rain. He always wants to know if it's going to rain "tomorrow." He gets upset if it is going to be sunny. Lately, we all have agreed that when he asks, it is just better to tell him there's a chance of rain. That answer satisfies him! When it does rain or storm, Isaac goes around the house shutting off all the lights and just watches intently out the windows! So if you ever need something to visit about with Isaac, talk about the weather and remember that there's always a chance of rain!

21

Isaac loves soda. He loves any kind of soda. He loves to watch it being poured into a glass and see the bubbles rise to the top. He is particularly tickled if he has to hurry and get a drink before the glass overflows. We have tried and tried over the last three years to have him cut down on soda. We have tried sparkling flavored water and other options but he just isn't happy with them. He often greets people by saying "no soda!"—his way of telling you that he shouldn't have so much soda. And then he may tell you "one soda a day." It is very important to him, which is why I believe he brings it up so often. He does still drink it, but we are having him try and cut down. It is such a difficult item to take away from him. It is one of his great joys!

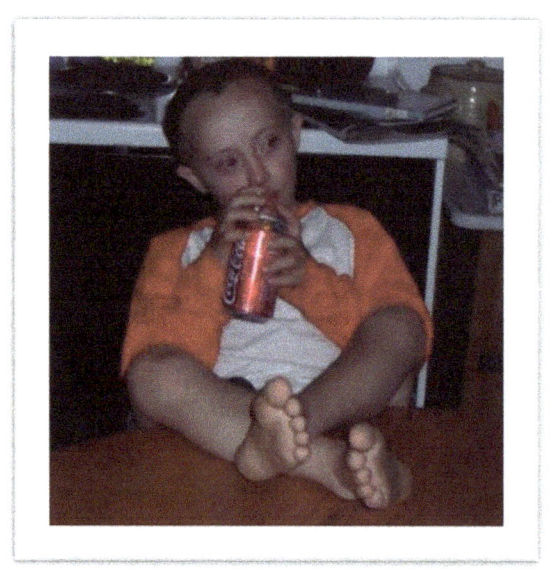

Isaac enjoying a soda!

22

Isaac has had speech therapy for nearly his entire life. He still receives weekly speech therapy at school. For the last few years, a focus of his therapy has been improving his conversation skills and encouraging him to use more complete sentences. With reminders, he can do it; however, he prefers to use "his language," which is comprised of two to three word statements or responses, and we have to fill in the gaps. His phrases are effective, but we would like to improve on it!

When he has a conversation with someone, he states the main idea and looks to me (or whichever family member is with him) to "interpret" and explain what he wants to say. For instance, lately he tells people his "pounds are bad," and then I have to explain that he is trying to lose weight. Or he may say "Barkley rash better," and I fill in that our dog, Barkley, has had a rash but it's getting better. And he EXPECTS an interpretation! He calls me out if I don't interpret exactly what he wants!

Those of us who spend time with Isaac have also come to affectionately use his phrases or "Isaacisms." When he has to go to the restroom: "potty bad." When he's hungry: "hungry bad." When he's thirsty: "thirsty bad." If he doesn't like something: "hate it." If I ask him how his supper is: "yep" (meaning good or fine).

One phrase that he has begun using in the last couple of years is "Ess _____," meaning "it's/I'm _____." Our family finds ourselves using this one too much! "Ess late," "ess raining!" "ess hot," "ess tired," and "ess aggravating." We have even turned it into a verb! (You are "essing" too much!) I admit that Isaac's speech is difficult to understand. Please always feel free to ask if you aren't sure what he's saying. But don't be surprised if he's just telling you that someone had gas or the dogs rash is better!

23

Isaac has very flat feet. This is fairly common in people who have Down syndrome. In mild cases, the heel rotates so that the person is walking on the inside of the heel. Flat feet result in heavy calluses of the feet, pointing of the front part of the feet away from each other (the opposite of being pigeon-toed) or even the creation of bone spurs. Isaac has tried orthotics over the years, with some success. He had X-rays of his feet a few years ago, and the doctor felt the only option was to surgically break and reset many bones in his feet. No thanks! I can't imagine Isaac trying to recover from that!

Often, Isaac's gait looks like he's trudging or plodding along. Sometimes I feel walking is a big effort for him. Isaac doesn't enjoy wearing shoes. As soon as he arrives home from anywhere, he takes his shoes and socks off. He would go barefoot year-round if possible! Not connected to being flat-footed, but another characteristic of Isaac's feet is the large gap between his big toe and second toe. This is also a common trait in people with Down syndrome. Funny how an extra chromosome in each cell of the body can make such unique characteristics!

24

There is a 50 to 100 percent incidence of obstructive sleep apnea in people with Down syndrome, with almost 60 percent of children with Down syndrome having abnormal sleep studies by age three to five years old. The overall incidence of sleep apnea increases as children get older. In Isaac's case, the apnea is caused by his low muscle tone in the mouth and upper airway, a larger tongue, and narrow airways in midface and throat. Being a little overweight also contributes to it, but in Isaac's case, it is primarily his anatomy.

Isaac had his first sleep study when he was four. Amazingly, he tolerated the sleep study quite well and has continued to do so each year. Isaac has severe obstructive sleep apnea. He had his tonsils and adenoids removed when he was four but that wasn't enough to make a difference for him.

He began using a BiPAP machine when he was five and has been a super trooper with it! He doesn't fully exhale so this machine also assists with pushing an exhale out. He had a period of time when he also used oxygen at night but that isn't currently necessary. At his sleep study last fall, the results indicated he had in excess of 120 apnea events in the first HOUR of the study—pretty severe. (Tech actually called the pulmonologist three times for guidance.) He should always use his BiPAP when sleeping, no napping on the couch. He quits breathing too often. There have been times when he has gone without it due to illness or severe congestion, and it is incredible to see the effects of a night without it.

Even with his machine, Isaac still experiences apnea episodes (and so do I, as his alarms sometimes go off five to six times per night), but we are thankful for this technology and thankful that Isaac tolerates this treatment.

25

What do I do with a seventeen-year-old during summer vacation? I take him to work with me, of course! First, let me say that I'm fortunate enough to have a job where I'm able to take Isaac with me, otherwise, I would be in search for a "babysitter" for Isaac, and finding a sitter for an adult with Down syndrome is a little different than finding a sitter for typical kids. He requires constant supervision, needs help in the bathroom, needs assistance getting food, and would be a huge safety risk if left unattended. It is just not possible, and I never see a time in the future that he will be able to stay by himself. (Hats off to my bosses, Paul Reither and Sally Stock, for allowing this to be possible.)

During summer vacation and on days off from school, Isaac gets up early and heads to work with me. While at the office, he has a schedule of tasks that he completes. I have made him a list that he follows, and he does his work without complaints and is usually quiet and respectful and causes no problems for those of us actually trying to work!

Isaac's tasks include assessing the weather, doing a stack of one hundred math flashcards with a calculator, doing domino math, writing his name five times, stringing beads on pipe cleaners (must put blue beads on blue pipe cleaners, red on red, green on green, etc.), sort colored paper clips and attach them to the corresponding paint sample card of the same color, sort a tray of colored craft pom-poms and isolate them with tongs and put them away in a divided box, and use a calculator and complete math worksheets.

He takes his work quite seriously! He usually finishes these jobs by noon, goes to lunch with us, and then is allowed to use his iPad in the afternoon—with headphones! I think he enjoys going to work because it is a routine, and he gets to see a few people. He does have some quirks about the office. Every time Paul's cell phone goes off, Isaac mocks the ringtone; when Paul sneezes, Isaac blesses him politely on the first sneeze, but the blessing gains more exasperation with each subsequent sneeze; and every time the office phone rings, Isaac says "Briggs Appraisals!" to imitate whoever answers the phone.

Isaac likes to run errands if anyone will take him, he's been to Kiwanis with us, and the highlight is visiting with our office neighbors!

It may slow down my productivity somewhat, but all in all, it has been a great experience to have Isaac at the office as our "intern"!

Isaac doing his work at Mom's office

26

Over the years, Isaac has experienced several losses of close family members or loved ones. He has a couple of unique ways of keeping these people in his memory. At family gatherings or mealtimes, Isaac concludes the family prayer with a recitation of the "roll of the dead" wherein he recites and blesses all of those close to him who have passed away. It usually begins something like this, "God bless Papa Wayne, Gramma Lil, Squint, Jennifer…" and his list goes on. He is very inclusive in his list.

Another way he continues to remember his loved ones is with pictures. Our family jokingly refers to this as his "portable shrine." He has several pictures in frames that he carries around the house, and he also brings them on car rides to school, church, or anywhere really. We discourage him from taking his pictures in to school, church, etc., as we think it becomes too much of a distraction for him. He talks to the pictures, he sets them up to play bingo with him, brings them to the table to eat with us, and generally includes them as if these photos were actually alive.

When he talks to the photos, I sometimes actually believe it is a two-way conversation. I will hear him talking to a picture and then I will say, "What did Papa Wayne say?" and usually he will respond with, "Good boy, Isaac" or some other phrase that my dad would have said to him.

Although many of these losses occurred several years ago, Isaac often experiences and expresses times of extreme sadness about these losses, just like any of us. He will have serious tears and wailing and say it is a "sad thing." He's right. He knows about heaven, he knows that his loved ones are there, and he's not afraid to discuss it. It is comforting to me that he is remembering his loved ones and connecting with them in a very real way.

SOMETHING EXTRA

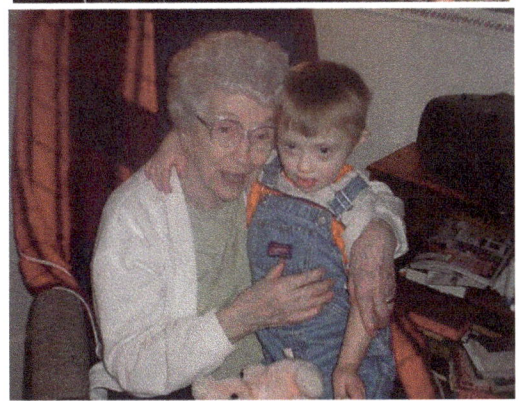

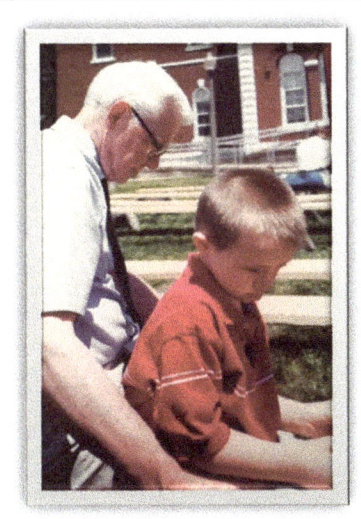

Isaac and Papa Wayne

57

27

Birthday parties, play dates, and other activities or outings can be tricky areas for families who have a child with a diagnosis or disability. The socialization aspect of these events is an important part of any child's development.

If a typical child is having an event where he invites the entire class, it can create questions of "Should I invite Isaac?" "What will Isaac do when he's here?" etc. Here's my "advice" (for what it's worth): if you are inviting everyone, invite Isaac! Don't be afraid to invite him. Feel free to call/contact me and say you are having an event and wanted to include Isaac. Even say, "If you would like to bring Isaac and stay that would be fine!"

Isaac would love to be included in events, but he is sort of a "plus-one" guest. I can't just drop Isaac off and come pick him up three hours later! I don't want parents to feel responsible for him or the uncertainty he brings. You are having the party; it shouldn't be your worry about watching Isaac.

Don't allow your worry or fear about him being there be the reason he wouldn't be on the guest list. But he needs constant supervision so he wouldn't do something to hurt himself, eat something that could cause him to choke, or act inappropriate. Don't be afraid to talk to parents and ask questions!

From my perspective as Isaac's mom, I would have LOVED for Isaac to be included, and I would welcome questions or the offer to stay at the event and keep an eye on Isaac and allow him the opportunity to socialize. He wants to be included!

28

Isaac enjoys taking car rides, particularly if there is going to be a stop for a drink or snack. He claims the front seat always. Once he is in his spot and has his seat belt fastened, he goes through a sort of pre-trip inspection wherein he tests to make sure his window goes up and down, tests the locks, and turns the fan on. Then he gets the radio adjusted and finds his CD and gets "The Chicken Dance" started, and that would be song number one.

No matter our destination, he feels the best music to listen to is "The Chicken Dance," repeating the introduction of it four times, then finally allowing it to play through, and then repeating it until we arrive at our destination. There are a couple other songs on his CD that he will randomly select, but our traveling tune is always "The Chicken Dance."

A few years ago as Isaac started getting bigger, he was often leaning forward and nearly blocking my view out the passenger window, so I worked with him about leaning back when we get to stop signs. Took a while, but he finally caught on that he must lean back against his seat at stop signs so I can see. He's very good at this! It was around this same time that I noticed other drivers were going out of turn when at stop intersections. It wasn't a coincidence. Isaac was motioning cars to take their turn. He had been watching me, so he thought he'd do it too. I quickly put a stop to that.

He will never be a licensed driver. I'm sure there are probably some individuals with Down syndrome who are capable of driving, but Isaac's level of development, coordination, reflexes, and many other reasons prohibit him from being a licensed driver. We have let him do steering at our house in our driveway area, and he can do some steering of the gator, but he doesn't do any of the footwork. He is very content being a passenger, as long as he's in front!

29

Every cell of the body has a nucleus where genetic material is stored in genes. Genes carry the codes responsible for all of our inherited traits. Typically, the nucleus contains twenty-three pairs of chromosomes, half from each parent. Down syndrome occurs when an individual has a full or partial extra copy of the twenty-first chromosome.

There are actually three types of Down syndrome. Keep reading because it really is sort of fascinating that this happens!

1. *Trisomy 21 (nondisjunction).*

   Down syndrome is usually caused by an error in cell division called nondisjunction. This results in an embryo with three copies of the twenty-first chromosome instead of two. Prior to or at conception, a pair of twenty-first chromosomes in either the sperm or egg fails to separate. As the embryo develops, the extra chromosome is replicated in EVERY CELL of the body. Ninety-five percent of Down syndrome cases are trisomy 21. This is the type Isaac has.

2. *Mosaic Down syndrome occurs in about 1 percent of Down syndrome cases.*

   This type is when there is a mixture of typical cells and cells with an extra chromosome. Some have the extra twenty-first chromosome and some don't. Some research suggests that a person who has Mosaic Down syndrome may have fewer characteristics of Down syndrome.

SOMETHING EXTRA

3. *Translocation Down syndrome makes up about 4 percent of the cases of Down syndrome.*

   The total number of chromosomes in the cells is forty-six; however, an additional full or partial copy of the twenty-first chromosome attaches itself (translocates) to another chromosome. The presence of the extra full or partial twenty-first chromosome causes the characteristics of Down syndrome.

Just what is in this twenty-first chromosome that causes these similar features and characteristics in this population? I find it so interesting that the genetic material can cause almond-shaped eyes, a flat profile, a singular crease on a palm of the hand, low muscle tone, and other characteristics unique to Down syndrome. These individuals are most certainly, fearfully, and wonderfully made!

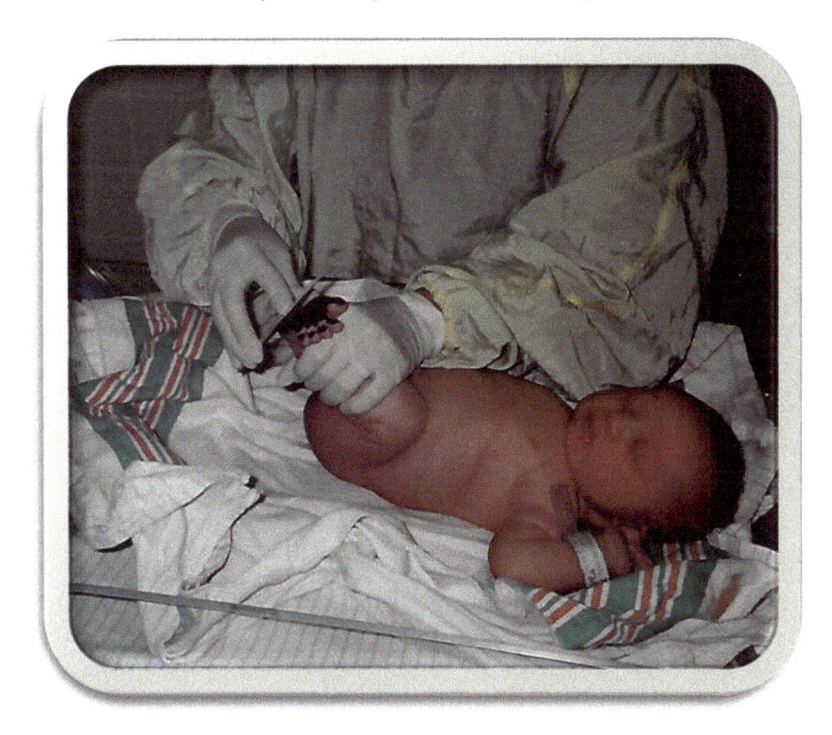

Isaac: December 10, 1998

30

It is certainly NOT Isaac's favorite thing to do, but he can write his name independently, and he does have some reading ability. I don't believe either of these skills are very meaningful to him. I think he wonders, "What's the point?"

Most of his "reading" is memorization using sight words he knows. I think he looks at the shapes of the words and the first letters of words. He likes to look through a couple of my music books and will show me a song he wants me to play, and somehow he knows the title, so he IS reading it or anyway recognizes the words.

He also will look at my phone when it rings and tell me who is calling, so he recognizes names in print. As far as writing goes, he will copy writing, but he doesn't spell words on his own. If we tell him what letters to write, he will do it (not happily)! He can do his name on his own though. His hands are weak, his coordination is poor, and he just isn't able to make his fingers work properly. My opinion on his lack of writing/coloring skills (and his lack of many fine motor skills) is that he didn't receive adequate occupational therapy at school.

He had an OT who worked with him (not happily!), and Isaac "tested" her patience (turned off lights, acted silly, made noises) and finally in second grade, the therapist said she couldn't work with him and put herself on a "consult basis." She obviously didn't make a good first impression on Isaac, and he knew how to "push her buttons." So Isaac has not had any occupational therapy since that time. All of the fine motor skills he does have are thanks to the creativity of his teachers and 1:1 aides. Oh, to think of the skills he could have if he would have received OT!

SOMETHING EXTRA

Interestingly, she is the only therapist Isaac has ever had who refused to work with him. He has had the same speech therapist all through grade school and high school, and she has never had any issues working with him.

Below are some samples of his typical handwriting.

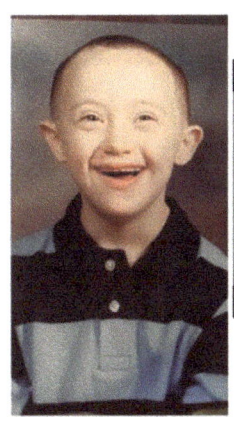

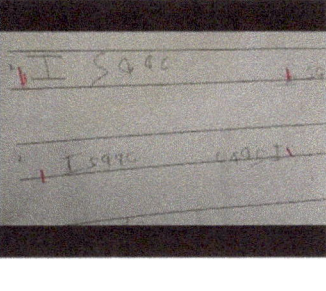

Isaac and Charlie doing homework

63

31

I would think it would be an unusual feeling to be a four-year-old inside a seventeen-year-old's body. I'm sure it would be a surreal experience for you or me. That is what Isaac is living in right now. I don't know if he is aware of it. I think he has many feelings of a typical seventeen-year-old yet many feelings of a much younger child.

It's a struggle within him, probably on things he doesn't and can't understand. The dichotomy of the four-year-old and the seventeen-year-old. The four-year-old in him loves to watch *Barney* and *Sesame Street* videos, likes to snuggle with "mommy," loves to blow bubbles outside. The seventeen-year-old in him doesn't like to be told "no more food," doesn't like to be told it's time for bed, loves to correct/try to discipline his little brother.

I believe he feels the emotions of a wide range of ages, and I'm sure it is sometimes difficult for him to understand what he is feeling or why he is feeling it. The four-year-old in him doesn't really know how to handle seventeen-year-old emotions, and that is sometimes a difficult issue. He likes to be like other guys his age, but he's not. Isaac's disposition is usually cheery, but he is experiencing many typical teenage emotions, which can bring about some moodiness or defiance. When the four-year-old in him has a meltdown about bedtime or a routine change, it is becoming more difficult to deal with the seventeen-year-old physical body he has. He's strong, and he's a teenager! Gotta say though, I'm glad he still likes to snuggle on the couch, and I'm hoping he always will.

SOMETHING EXTRA

Isaac enjoying snuggles with Daddy Matt and Charlie

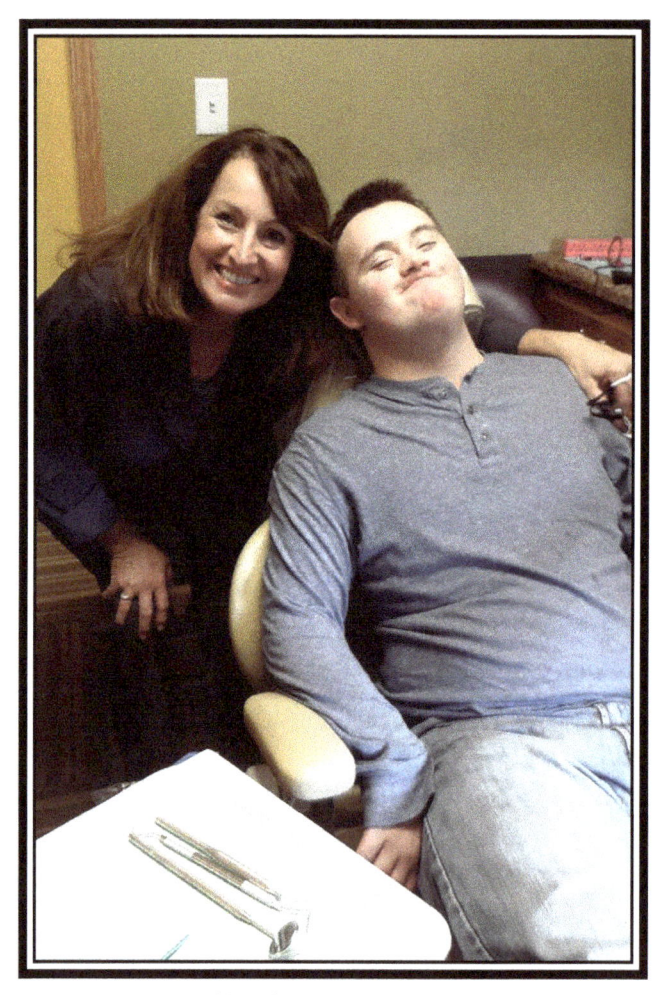

Isaac and his dentist, Dr. Becky Canter

32

Isaac had a dental appointment yesterday, and I was reminded of what a great dentist he has! Isaac has been going to Rebecca Canter (at Beardstown Family Dental) for probably ten years, and he LOVES going to the dentist!

Having Down syndrome hasn't caused any serious dental issues for Isaac. He was late getting his teeth, they didn't arrive in the typical order, and he is missing some permanent teeth (never had them). His teeth are quite small, and he doesn't show them often. He grinds them while sleeping and occasionally while awake.

Often people with Down syndrome are at an increased risk for gum disease due to an impaired immune system, but this hasn't been an issue for Isaac. We have been very fortunate to have Dr. Canter and each member of her amazing staff provide Isaac's dental care. It takes patience, creativity, enthusiasm, and a love for your job to provide dental care for someone like Isaac. The hygienists have to be so specific in giving their instructions. Typical patients know when to open/close their mouths, but when they work with Isaac, they have to tell him every move they need him to make. X-rays are a particular challenge!

From the moment Isaac walks into the door at the dentist office, he is pampered! The ladies always remember his interests and make great conversation with him, and usually several of the hygienists stop in just to visit with him and share a laugh with him. They always treat him like a prince! No wonder he loves going to the dentist!

33

Many people often think that only "older" women have babies with Down syndrome. While the incidence of births of babies with Down syndrome does increase with the mother's age, more babies are born to women under the age of thirty-five due to higher fertility rates. Simply put, most babies with Down syndrome are born to women under the age of thirty-five because younger women have more babies than older women.

Actually about 80 percent of babies with Down syndrome are born to women under the age of thirty-five. I was twenty-nine years old when Isaac was born. Many of the moms who guided me through the first years of Isaac's life were also young moms.

The current statistics of mother's age and chances of having a baby with Down syndrome are as follows: age 20=1 in 2,000; age 25=1 in 1,200; age 30=1 in 900; age 35=1 in 365; age 40=1 in 100; age 45=1 in 30.

I'm a mom who had a typical baby when I was twenty-three, had a baby with Down syndrome when I was twenty-nine, and then had a typical baby when I was forty-one. And yes, I had prenatal testing with each pregnancy. With Isaac, I had the triple screen blood test, which showed a one in thirty-six chance of having a baby with Down syndrome. I then had an amniocentesis for confirmation and peace of mind so I could use the next five months of my pregnancy to prepare. That was the right decision for me. The prenatal testing when I was pregnant with Charlie was a bit more intense as I was an older mom and also already had a child with Down syndrome. Newer techniques and testing were available. It worked for me. What works for one may not work for another, but the testing I had gave me the opportunity to research and prepare as best I could for the circumstances Isaac would bring.

34

It is not uncommon for people with Down syndrome to have sensory issues, meaning their nervous system receives the messages from their senses but may not know how to interpret them, may interpret them at a delayed rate, or may not make an appropriate response. Isaac indeed has some sensory issues, and I will try to explain a few.

As a small boy, he would be overstimulated and need to "calm" down. There could be too many things happening at once around him and his senses were "overloaded," which would then cause him to need calming (or there was too little stimulation going on for his body and he needed "input").

The most successful ways to calm Isaac were as follows: lay him in a large (5'x5') piece of spandex; have two people pick it up on the ends and swing it back and forth; have him wear a weighted vest; "brush" his arms and legs with a surgical scrub brush; do joint compressions beginning in his knuckles, then wrists, elbows, shoulders, etc. All of these remedies were prescribed by his occupational therapist, and they truly worked to settle him down and relax him. The OT explained that his body needed reassurance and pressure because otherwise he probably felt like he was out of control or a bunch of loose nerves with no direction.

Other issues Isaac has related to this include an intolerance to some food textures (Jell-O, mashed potatoes), a constant need for holding beads and rubbing them/swinging them, a need for holding or swinging a white dishtowel, an obsession with the front part of his hair (rubbing/pulling it). He also likes to "chew" or bite on part of his hand and often will make a steady growling or clicking noise when he's tired or needs rest. Some of these may have turned into obsessions/behaviors, but they are related to his senses and what he needs to comfort or soothe himself.

We all have varying levels of what we can tolerate as an acceptable level or type of sensation. Some people can't stand loud noises, having a hat on their head, the feeling of socks slipping down, etc. But typical people can EXPRESS the frustration, identify what is causing it, and resolve it. Isaac can't do this. He is unable to identify and express what is causing a sensory issue for him.

I often feel it is during these times of sensory frustration for him that he will misbehave. He knows something isn't right but can't express it. Something may be too loud, clothing may be too tight or too itchy, someone may be in his personal space, he may be overwhelmed somehow so he begins to "unravel" and seek some sort of relief, whether it is making a repetitive noise, swinging his towel, rubbing his hair, or playing with his beads. These are his self-calming remedies, and we know when we see an increase in these that something has been bothering him.

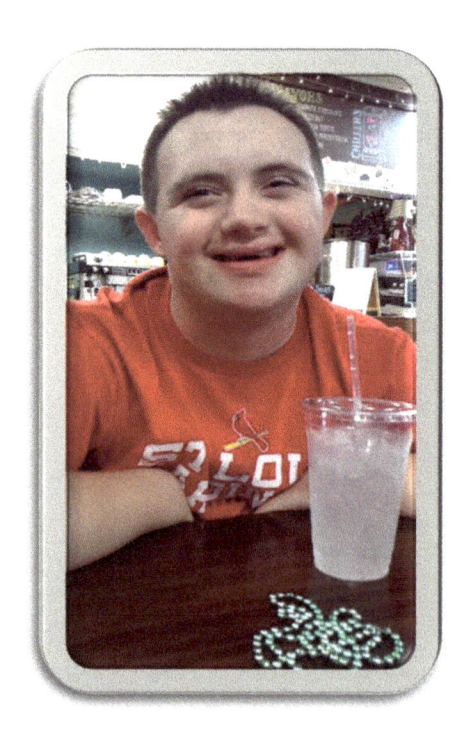

35

Isaac has always had a local primary care physician who has provided him with OUTSTANDING care. She has always gone out of her way to care for him, research topics that pertain to Down syndrome, and treat every aspect of Isaac's health. In addition to his local provider, Isaac annually goes to the Down syndrome clinic at St. Louis Children's Hospital. This is a comprehensive appointment where Isaac gets evaluations in cardiology, ENT, pulmonology, hematology, physical therapy, occupational therapy, speech therapy, audiology, and nutrition. It is sort of a one-stop shop. These providers specialize in Down syndrome, but they only see Isaac once a year. Isaac's local provider knows HIM and his specific behaviors and personality. I feel the combination of his local provider and an annual visit to the Down syndrome clinic provides Isaac with the best possible medical care.

There have been instances when we have had to take Isaac to get emergency medical care at a hospital, and we have not always had good experiences due to staff not knowing how to communicate with Isaac or knowing how to "handle" him. (Disclaimer: before it sounds like I'm slamming the medical community, I'm not! He has received good treatment, but often hospital staff has had limited exposure to people like Isaac so they just don't know how to deal with his abilities.)

Here are examples of some of the "not-so-good experiences": an X-ray tech attempting to get a chest X-ray but being very frustrated and visibly irritated that Isaac didn't know how to hold his breath and hold still; staff being irritated that Isaac doesn't keep his mouth closed over the thermometer; irritated that Isaac doesn't know how to give a specimen and can't do it on demand; staff irritated that Isaac can't answer questions about how long he has had symptoms; and just not giving Isaac the time and attention he deserves.

When he was having a CT scan recently, the techs said they "could handle it" and wanted me to wait outside. I suggested they may need to be very specific about their instructions and say them in very simple terms, and if they needed him to lay still they would have to tell him that. They just assumed he would know. (They ended up saying, "Maybe you better come in." Ya think?)

It has sometimes felt like some staff really just doesn't want to deal with Isaac, and I'd hate to think that is because of him having Down syndrome.

He has had some good experiences where ER staff/techs go out of their way to explain exactly what they needed Isaac to do, demonstrated how Isaac needs to do something like hold his breath or make a fist so they can get blood easier or find creative ways to get him to do what they need or even get him a soda when he keeps talking about a drink! Hats off to these folks who understand that Isaac isn't a typical patient and are willing to work harder and more creatively to give him appropriate care.

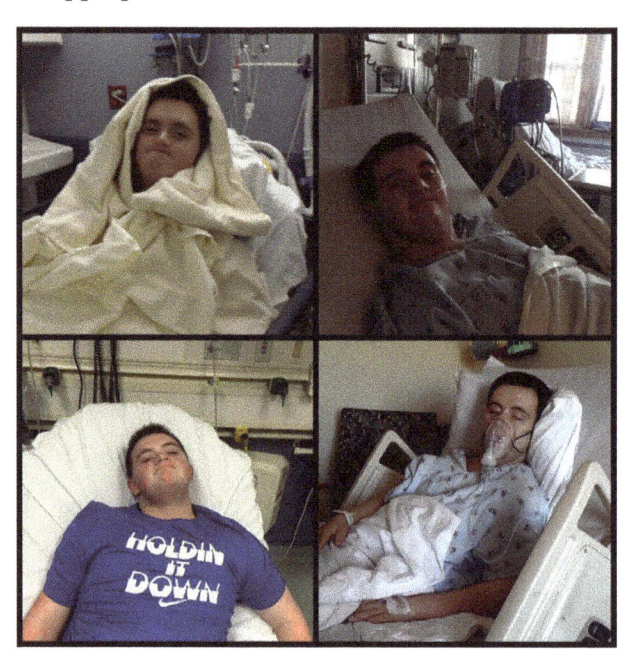

36

Isaac enjoys social events and being around people. He seems to be everyone's buddy! He tends to be most comfortable around adults, though, as opposed to his teenage peers. I know he enjoys being around his peers and is excited, but his comfort level is highest when he's with his teachers, his aide, the janitors, his parents, or adult relatives. Part of it may be that he senses adults are more at ease with HIM than peers are—and that is understandable. He doesn't have the opportunity to spend time with peers except at school.

I've taken him to high school sporting events and encouraged him to sit with the students, but so far, he chooses to sit with me instead. I sometimes feel sad for him that he doesn't really have "friends" and doesn't have a social life (except for tagging along everywhere with family). It is more like parallel friendships rather than inclusive friendship. But I never fault his peers for this, as I completely understand that it would be a huge responsibility to include Isaac in social outings. He can be unpredictable or impulsive, he would need constant supervision and interpreting, he could have a meltdown, he could act too silly, and it could just be difficult for peers to handle him. I do believe that at some point in the future, probably once he finishes high school, he will begin going on social outings. For now, I'm thankful that he has supportive teachers and staff at school, for he truly is delighted to be around them!

37

We have a family pet at our house, Barkley. Barkley is a six-year-old St. Bernard and quite large. She is young at heart and loves to jump on us, which nearly knocks us over! She is very energetic and playful but does not realize her own strength.

Isaac LOVES Barkley and for some reason, Barkley doesn't really jump on Isaac or maul him like she does the rest of us. If Barkley were to jump on Isaac, I'm certain he would fall down, as his balance would give way, and he isn't strong enough to withstand Barkley's weight. But Barkley calms down for Isaac, as if she knows Isaac couldn't tolerate her jumping/playfulness. They seem to understand each other or at least have some sort of arrangement between them.

Isaac talks to Barkley every day, and in good weather, he sits in a chair on our patio and just pets her and visits her, and Barkley enjoys it! Isaac loves to talk about Barkley! He loves to know where she is, what she's doing, and generally loves keeping an eye on her out the window! He's always very concerned about what Barkley is doing. They are great buddies, and I marvel at the respect they have for each other.

38

Music is a very important part of Isaac's life. He appreciates MANY genres of music and listens daily to his favorites. Anyone who knows Isaac very well, knows he LOVES "The Chicken Dance" and that is usually his traveling music for the car. We listen to it EVERY DAY REPEATEDLY on the way to/from school (that is thirty-six miles worth of polka music daily!).

Isaac prefers to be sung to while having his teeth brushed, and that music is always "Hallelu, Hallelu." While our family is getting ready in the morning, he usually blares the "Sabre Dance" which is actually kind of appropriate as we are scurrying furiously to be on time somewhere. I would say his top ten list is as follows:

10. Magic (Ben Folds)
9. I Gotta Feeling (Black Eyed Peas)
8. How Great Thou Art (Carrie Underwood)
7. Our House (Crosby, Stills Nash and Young)
6. 100 Years (Five for Fighting)
5. Carry On (Fun)
4. Sing After Me (Madeline Kahn and Grover from *Sesame Street*)/Jellyman Kelly (James Taylor)
3. Wake Up Call (Maroon 5)
2. The Book of Love (Peter Gabriel)
1. It is Well With My Soul Medley (Amy Grant)

Those are his "go-to" songs. He LOVES Christmas carols, and many years we listen to them year-round. He also has a very emotional connection to several hymns including: "Majesty," "Eagle's

Wings," "Here I Am Lord," "How Great Thou Art," "Lord of the Dance," and "It is Well With My Soul."

Isaac enjoys singing in church and making his joyful noise. He doesn't always know all the words, but he sings from deep down in his heart with raw emotion. When he sings, I truly believe he is feeling the presence of God.

At home, he asks me to play the piano for him every day. He brings me music books and opens them to the songs he wants, and then I play and he stands up, beads in hand, and sways and sings his heart out.

There are times when I selfishly just don't want to play the piano because I have other things I need to be doing. But I do it for him, and I'm always glad I did. He has a way of bringing a peace to me when he is singing, and it allows me to escape for just a few moments while I listen to him. Isaac is connected to God through his music, and I treasure being able to be a witness.

39

Isaac and his little brother, Charlie, tend to tease and bicker like typical brothers. But they tease and bicker differently than typical six- and seventeen-year-old siblings. Their level of teasing is much lower. I know it is sometimes frustrating for Charlie to have a brother who has Down syndrome, but he handles it well for the most part. I recently had a talk with Charlie and just tried asking his thoughts about having an older brother with Down syndrome. Below are Charlie's thoughts in his own words:

"Sometimes I wonder what it would be like to have a brother who doesn't have Down syndrome. I love that Isaac is nice. Lots of people always come up and talk to him. He likes to sing. He's got a good voice. I have to do things for Isaac like help him with his shoes or coat and hold his hand to cross a street. Sometimes, I think mom and dad are harder on me than they are on Isaac. It's okay that Isaac has Down syndrome 'cause I already got a normal sister. God made Isaac this way because he wanted me to have a brother like that. It's hard when Isaac gets sad or upset. I don't like his loud crying. I wish he could drive so he could take me go school!"

Yes, I'd say they are pretty typical brothers!

40

Isaac is VERY excited about his upcoming eighteenth birthday (December 10). He keeps saying, "Almost 18!" and he has a countdown in his school notebook so he knows how many days till the big day.

He has made a list of MANY people he wants to invite to a party. This is a big deal to him! Most kids have something special they want for their birthday, and usually, it is a big item and something different each year. Not Isaac. He asks for the same thing EVERY year (for birthday and Christmas). He always wants soda, ketchup, pickles, potato chips, grape jelly, chocolate pudding, ranch dressing, and sometimes M&M, body spray, and shower gel.

This year, he has added jalapeño poppers to his list! He actually is disappointed if he doesn't get these items. He is an easy person to shop for, but I always feel guilty because I just buy him groceries and when his birthday is over, and his gifts are eaten, he's really got nothing to show for it—no lasting gifts.

But I feel like Isaac really lives in the moment and doesn't give any thought to the future. He is happy with the present time and doesn't lose any of that happiness worrying about tomorrow. Truly I don't feel he has any concept of time, so the future isn't even a consideration to him.

Many times when he wakes up in the morning, he says something like, "Here I am! I'm back!" as if he went to bed and thought that would be the end, but he wakes up and IS back again to have another day, and he's EXCITED about it! I don't believe he has any expectation of tomorrow. It is, after all, not promised. I'm a bit jealous that he can do that, not worry about the future. I worry about everything, and then I worry some more about everything else that could possibly happen. Not Isaac. He lives for today and enjoys it! No worries. When we celebrate on December 10, I'll be buying his groceries for him because it makes him so happy, and he can use them "today" because today is the gift.

Isaac and his annual birthday gifts

41

Isaac has been involved with Special Olympics in Beardstown for almost ten years. This program has provided amazing opportunities for Isaac: advancement in coordination and athletic skills, development of friendships with teammates, social activities, and an opportunity for family to gather and support and cheer on Isaac.

Isaac's athletic skills have greatly improved over the years. He participates in track and basketball. For his track season, he has competed in the one hundred-meter run, standing long jump, and the softball throw. This year, he tried bowling for the first time (just practice, not competition) and will likely try it again next year.

Special Olympics has been a great activity for Isaac and our family. When he has competitions, he usually has a large fan club of followers, and he loves to see his supporters. It has also rewarded our family by introducing us to a whole new population of fantastic people—his teammates. Our family has grown to love his teammates, rally and support them, and truly enjoy being their fans.

The Special Olympics program has opened our hearts to include some of the greatest, most inspiring folks we know. I encourage anyone who wants to witness true sportsmanship, determination, and love of sports to attend a competition of Special Olympics. It is a refreshing take on athletic competitions. Support your local program whenever you have the opportunity!

SOMETHING EXTRA

JILL ROEGGE

42

Expecting a child is a time of dreaming and wondering what the new child will be like. I was given a huge advantage during my pregnancy when I found out that Isaac would have Down syndrome. Yes, I had a new set of worries and unknowns, but I still had dreams for him.

Prenatal testing is controversial but also helpful. I've said it before, and I will reiterate: prenatal testing can diagnose many serious medical conditions, yet there are many things you can't get a prenatal diagnosis for which are, in my opinion, much worse (being a brat, being a bully, having a bad sense of humor, having no empathy, having no conscience).

To me, Down syndrome is the Cadillac of disabilities, and I'm forever grateful to God that Isaac is healthy and is as "abled" as he is. Is it challenging? Is it stressful? Is it tiring that I must do all the self-care tasks for a seventeen-year-old boy? Yes, but so is parenting a "typical child."

Every parent has stress and challenges, just in different ways. Isaac is not always happy. He is not always angelic. He is often tricky and ornery. I'm not always a great mom. I lose my patience. I get frustrated with the incessant routines. But we make it! This extra chromosome that is in every cell of Isaac's body has caused us to be connected to some extra special people—people we may not have known otherwise.

Isaac has been surrounded by incredibly caring, compassionate, encouraging family members and supporters who always seem to appear when we need them most. It is not a coincidence. It is God's plan that these folks are along on our journey, and hopefully, they are blessed along the way.

43

After school, I raced the boys home to change them into their Halloween costumes so we could make it to Gramma Judy's and back to other relatives in Arenzville. Charlie as an Indian and Isaac as a hot dog, for the sixth year in a row. It's a classic.

On our way to gramma's house, Isaac was drinking a diet Dr. Pepper. When we arrived at grammas to trick or treat, I told him he needed to leave it in the car when he went to the door. This didn't make him happy at all. A small argument ensued, and I finally compromised in my frustrations and said that I would carry the soda. So I put his bottle of soda in my coat pocket and brought it with us to trick or treat because you just might work up a thirst after knocking on one door and need a drink of soda.

Content with that compromise, Isaac proceeded to Gramma Judy's door and excitedly exclaimed "trick or treat" and received his annual full-sized Hershey bar. The trick was on me though, when gramma presented Isaac with a special brown paper bag with an extra treat inside, a can of diet Dr. Pepper, which he opened with lightning speed and guzzled in record time.

We visited for a few minutes since Isaac's thirst was quenched, and then set out to our next trick or treating destination—Uncle Ken and Aunt Marty's house. Isaac calls her Aunt Smarty. At their house, Isaac brought up several things he's been told not to talk about. Charles helped himself to multiple handfuls of candy. Isaac reminded us of several people who have passed away. He also brought up two of Ken and Marty's granddaughters, Kendra and Brooke, and wanted to know how they were doing. We took some photos, Charlie raced to the car, and I helped Isaac down the front porch steps and away we went to our next stop.

SOMETHING EXTRA

A quick trip into Uncle Kenny and Aunt Pat's house to trick or treat, and Isaac tried Charlie's method of grabbing several handfuls of candy. After a reprimand, he put some candy back and then reminded us all of departed loved ones. Charlie is impatiently waiting to get out of there and on to meet his friends at the park. We make a hasty exit, and I offer a quick threat to forgo the rest of trick or treating if whiny behavior doesn't improve. Off we go.

Ah, it is easy to trick or treat at Aunt Sally's house. She has her set up outside, and we don't have steps or breakables to worry about. We are not confined. Sally understands these trick or treaters and provides an easy place to be.

We meet some friends and head down Frederick Street. Charlie and his friends are ahead of Isaac and me, and I can hear their excited chatter and watch them run from house to house, getting at least two houses ahead of Isaac and me.

At each house, Isaac trudges up porch steps in his hot dog costume, pounds on doors and bellows "TRICK a TREAT!" Sometimes, a teenager answers the door and awkwardly hands their peer some candy. Sometimes an adult wearing a mask answers, and Isaac is taken aback.

A man in a Donald Trump costume hands out candy on one porch. Charlie runs from that house yelling, "We should vote for Donald Trump! I just talked to him!" Isaac poses with the Donald for a picture, having no clue who Donald even is.

At each stop, Isaac tells the homeowner thank you and also lets them know he hasn't eaten supper yet and that he wants to go to Dairy Queen. It is Monday, after all, and that's what Isaac does for supper on Mondays.

At each porch, I must help Isaac up the steps and offer even more assistance as he comes down the steps. He walks to many houses, but he has worked up quite the sweat, and I take him to his dad's porch at around 6:30 p.m. so he can finish out Halloween by handing out candy. He continues to ramble about no supper and Dairy Queen. I leave him there and continue on with Charlie, Matt, and our friends.

We finish our evening and head home with oodles of candy, some crankiness, and definitely tired. We leave Isaac to spend the night with his Dad. After we had been home for half an hour, my friend sends me a text that says, "Just saw Isaac at Dairy Queen. He seemed very happy to be there!"

Of course he was—it is Monday after all.

44

You know how you hear people seeing a newborn baby and tell the parents, "Oh, you make beautiful babies!" or "Oh, he's just perfect!" That sort of implies to the parents that THEY are responsible for, or THEY deserve the credit for making this beautiful/perfect baby. And I know that "technically," they are responsible for making it!

Following that line of thinking, I guess I'm responsible for having made Isaac an "imperfect" baby. Other people make perfect babies; I made an imperfect one! Now I want to shift the responsibility for a bit and say that God is the one who made those "perfect" babies so that would also mean that God made my "imperfect" baby.

Did God make a mistake? God created Isaac with an extra chromosome in EVERY CELL OF HIS BODY, which has completely altered his development. Is this a mistake? I cannot bring myself to believe God's creation of Isaac was a mistake. He purposefully created him with an extra copy of the twenty-first chromosome.

I often wonder what God's purpose was. I've bandied about many ideas over the years as to why Isaac was created this way and here are some of my thoughts: God knew I loved babies/toddlers so He gave me someone who will always be childlike, to ensure I would always be humbled, to teach me to stand up for the weak, to teach me compassion, to slow my life down, to help me appreciate the simple aspects of life, to learn to take my time and appreciate small victories, to teach me the importance of serving others, to connect me to people I may never have encountered except for a common interest in Down syndrome.

I can lay awake at night and ponder answers to my questions, and I can also emphatically proclaim that I do not believe Isaac is a mistake. I know our society often claims that God "made a mistake" in creating someone a certain way. And if people need to believe that in their specific case, that is certainly their prerogative. But God did not make a mistake when He made Isaac. God created Isaac this way on purpose, WITH purpose, and made him in His image.

What if we make it to heaven and everyone there has Down syndrome? Hey, it could happen! Psalm 139:14 says, "I praise you because I am fearfully and wonderfully made; your works are wonderful, I know that full well."

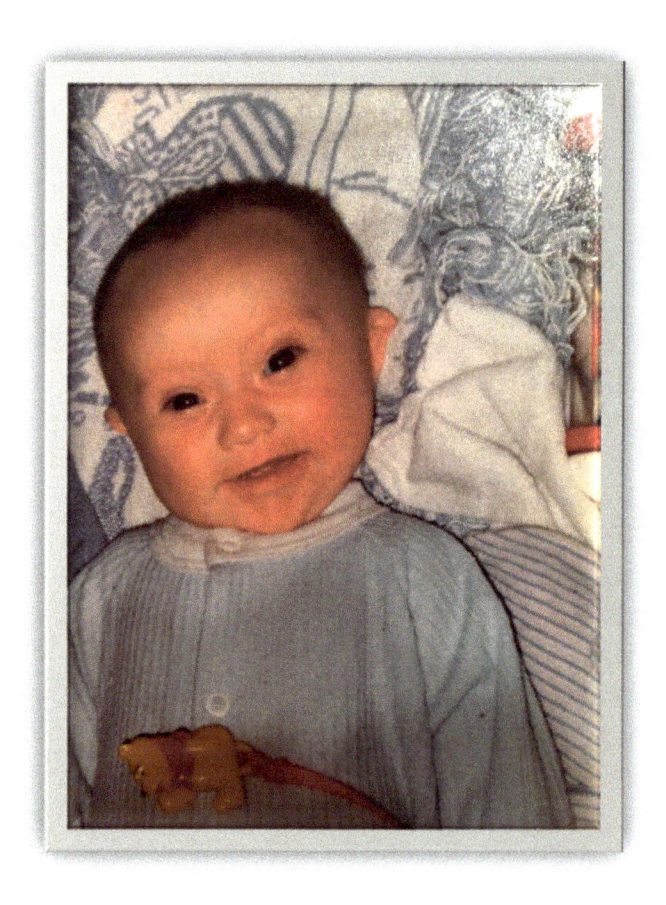

45

I feel people are typically most at ease around people who are similar to them in some ways. When I learned that the baby I was pregnant with had Down syndrome, I was not "at ease." I pretended I was so that everyone else would be accepting and be okay with who I was going to bring into this world.

I had grown up in Virginia, Illinois (population 1,800), at a time when there weren't many visible folks with disabilities. I had experienced very limited exposure to anyone who was developmentally delayed.

My mom had two adult cousins from Oklahoma, who visited maybe once a year, who had varying levels of what we called mental retardation (yeah, I grew up in the '70s/'80s!). And I had shared an annual supper with them and a bit of conversation, but I didn't truly KNOW people with disabilities. I'm somewhat ashamed to admit this, but during my pregnancy, I would actually get on the internet and search for pictures of people with Down syndrome. I would search for pictures of babies with Down syndrome. I was trying to get used to the "look" of Down syndrome, trying to see what I could be expecting, trying to give myself hope that this "different" person was going to look all right.

When Isaac arrived, he was my first "close encounter with a different kind." I would say I was fairly comfortable with him because he was mine, and I knew him from the moment he was born. I learned what I could expect from him. I learned about his physical features. I learned about what he could do.

As Isaac aged, I learned his language, his emotions, his habits, his mannerisms. I felt comfortable with HIM. I now had an advantage in the world of people with disabilities—or so I thought. Isaac began

Special Olympics when he was eight, and I met a whole new population of people—so many ages, abilities, diagnoses, so overwhelming!

I was comfortable with MY little boy with Down syndrome. I had known him his whole life! These were adults, and I had no clue how to interact with them. I was a little afraid of some of the people and didn't know how they would react to me. I was the outsider in this group. It made me want to fit in with them, learn about them, and become someone they would want to talk to, but I didn't really know how to break the ice with them. Isaac was my helper.

This new population of people all of a sudden wanted to be around me because they wanted to be around the little guy! I discovered that these people were so welcoming to me (the outsider). They had lots of questions for me. They wanted to tell me about themselves. They were interesting. They were somewhat unpredictable sometimes. They were fun!

I was nervous the first few times I was around the team, but I eventually felt at ease. As Isaac has continued participating in Special Olympics, I've become very comfortable around this different population of people. I look forward to seeing them at practices and events. I feel close to them and care deeply for them. It is interesting to me that I was afraid just because I hadn't been around people who were different than me.

I imagine many people feel this way. I think that people who know Isaac are fairly comfortable with him. They are used to him. He is "the one" they have experience with. But if they were to encounter a whole Special Olympians team, they would perhaps be overwhelmed, as I was at first. And that is completely understandable! It is difficult to break into a new group of people when we aren't used to the differences.

Now that it is 2017, we need to realize that people with disabilities/differences are going to be more visible in our society, perhaps working at a store or restaurant we visit. These folks are not to be kept hidden anymore; we will see them out and about! This may make some of us uncomfortable because we haven't been exposed to this population of people. It may push us out of our comfort zones, but if we make an effort with a smile, a "hi," a "hey, how's it going,"

SOMETHING EXTRA

we are breaking the ice and opening ourselves up to the possibility of learning about other people and enriching our lives. I'm the first to admit I was scared of the differences, but I will also be the first to admit that I'm thankful and privileged to be friends with people who are different than me.

Isaac and some of his Special Olympics teammates

46

Isaac is unreliable in providing answers. Often he answers a question with the response that will get the largest laugh from his audience. He is a performer. So when he visits a medical provider, I often have to screen his responses and add my editorial remarks. I'm not trying to speak FOR him, but I am trying to get the most accurate information to the provider as possible.

Isaac has had the same medical provider since he was about four years old and she knows him, understands him, and realizes that he can't verbalize many answers to medical questions and that we often must just observe him very closely to figure out what is wrong with him.

A medical provider can ask Isaac if his ears hurt and he will say yes. Then more questions are asked and a return to the ear question just moments later, and this time his answer is no. The only way to tell is to then look in his ears. He doesn't provide accurate information. There have been occasions when Isaac wasn't able to see his regular provider, and man, that is usually an awkward and comical (to me) situation.

One occasion was when he saw a doctor who was from India, and the language barrier on BOTH ends was just unbelievable. The doctor asked Isaac if he was eating well. Isaac was trying to tell the doctor that he has "trouble with the pork" (because he does have trouble chewing pork).

The doctor responded, "You like pork?"
Isaac said, "Trouble with the pork."
Doctor said, "Yes, pork."
Isaac responded, "Trouble with the pork."

I seriously looked around the room for hidden cameras because I felt like I was caught in one of those "who's on first?" scenes.

Isaac also had some "not-so-positive" experiences with medical providers. He was sent to have a chest X-ray, and the technicians were quite irritated with him because he wasn't standing still enough. He had a CT scan where he wasn't able to follow all of the instructions because he just doesn't understand the directions. They would ask if he understood, and he would say yes. Again, an unreliable answer.

When Isaac was hospitalized for five days last year with double pneumonia, I nearly decided to quit my job and become an advocate for people with special needs who are seeking medical care. If Isaac had been admitted to the hospital on his own, it would have taken days for them to determine what was wrong. People would ask him to rate his pain (remember Isaac's love of numbers?). He was asked to keep thermometers under his tongue (nearly impossible). He was asked where he was hurting. He was asked to describe the pain. He was asked if he had any tingling sensations. Tingling? What's tingling? He was asked to transfer from one bed to another. Transfer, really? He was asked if it felt worse doing certain activities. He was asked so many things that were completely beyond his comprehension, yet the staff wanted HIM to answer and were sometimes irritated if I tried to explain.

I would try and explain that I wasn't trying to "speak" for him but felt I could give them the best description of my observations, and it would save us all some time. But many of the staff wanted it to come from him, which I KNEW would be completely unreliable and most likely humorous.

Many times I would try and explain it to Isaac in simpler terms or terms I thought he may understand, hoping the staff would pick up on the need to change their vocabulary and consider that although the patient was eighteen, he was mentally four. I realize that medical professionals can't be expected to understand every possible condition that walks in for care, but there also needs to be a level of respect for the parent who is trying to "interpret" for the patient.

Parents of kids with special needs are absolute experts on their kids. Not to diminish the qualifications of the entire medical community, but as parents, we see the situation every day and know when something isn't quite right. Fortunately, our hospital stays have been few, and when Isaac was hospitalized, Lydia or I was with him twenty-four hours/day. I shudder to think of those individuals with disabilities who must travel the medical maze without an advocate or family member to assist in their diagnosis process and care.

As a side note, when Isaac was two, he was attending one of my medical appointments, and in small talk with the provider, we were discussing Down syndrome. The doctor asked if he would outgrow it.

If I ever retire, maybe I will begin a service to provide sensitivity training to medical providers. There is a need.

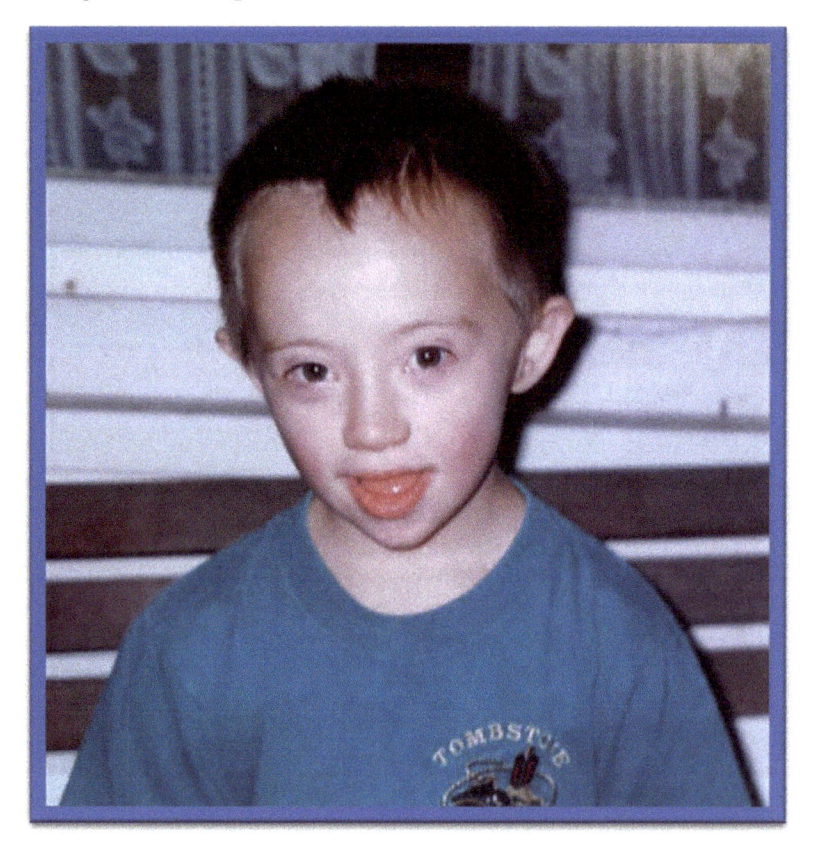

47

Isaac was a wanderer when he was younger. I think he could still be a wanderer if he was given the opportunity. Between the ages of about three to eight, Isaac liked to leave the house and not tell anyone. During this time period, we lived in town, and fortunately it was a small, friendly town. We supervised Isaac quite diligently, but he would still escape from the house. Sometimes he would walk down the street, sometimes he would walk two houses down to my sister's house, he would cross streets, and he would sit in the street.

I could run to the basement to switch a load of laundry and return, and he would be gone. I would frantically search the house, holler for him (he would NEVER answer), then head outside looking anywhere I thought he may go.

One day when Isaac was about three years old, a man knocked on our door holding Isaac and asked if he lived at this house. Isaac had escaped and was sitting in the street. The man honked at him, and Isaac just waved and made no attempt to move. Isaac wasn't able to intelligibly verbalize where he lived, but fortunately, the man came to our house first. We installed locks and upper chains on each of our doors. But we were a family with multiple members who were always going in/out and often a door could get left unlocked, and with locks and chains at the tops of all of our exits, we felt somewhat imprisoned in our own home. We eventually looked into a tracking device, which at that time was a rather new strategy and quite costly. We considered putting a bell on him so we would hear him but opted to put it on the doors instead. Thankfully, we lived in a small community where everyone knew Isaac and truly looked out for his well-being.

There were several neighbors who would return Isaac to us. Some will criticize the parenting that could allow a child to escape. I accept the criticism and challenge the critics to attempt to live in a household on "lockdown." I guess I could have sat in the same room with him and watched him for twenty-four hours a day, every day, or put him on some sort of tether, but none of that is living.

The stress that a wandering child puts on a family is incredible. We were not inattentive parents. We sought guidance from others who experienced a wanderer. We lost plenty of sleep due to the fear of Isaac getting up in the night and wandering. What if we didn't hear? I know I trained myself to sleep very lightly. As Isaac has aged, this problem has diminished. Given the opportunity though, I do believe he is capable of wandering again. Since we have been in the country, my fears have expanded to include the fear of him wandering into a field of mature corn.

There have been a few occasions where he has left the house to look at lightning or dark clouds. He doesn't tell me he's leaving. He walks as far west on our property as he can but stops at the edge of the field. He's just taking in the weather, smelling the air, and embracing the wind. When we go shopping or to places besides church, school, or relatives houses, Isaac has an "alert" bracelet to identify him, give our phone numbers, and alert that he is not able to answer questions accurately. (Back to him being unreliable, he may tell someone his name is "Pickle"!) I keep a firm hand on Isaac whenever we are in public, just in case he gets the urge to wander.

48

I'm always striving to treat my kids equally, providing them the same amount of love, affection, time, attention, and even material items. Well, I don't succeed across the board, but I try and feel that I do the best I can to meet each one's needs.

Recently, I have come to accept a reality that has always filled me with much guilt—attending events/taking a vacation WITHOUT Isaac. In order to "be fair," I always felt I needed to tow Isaac along with us wherever we went, and many times, it made our family miserable, especially Isaac. He enjoys going and doing things, but I don't feel like he really CARES about going places all the time. He is truly content to stay at home, go to gramma's or Sally's houses and have fun being "left behind."

Lots of times I think he would actually prefer to stay at home, but out of a mom's guilt, I've always dragged him along everywhere. I have struggled with this for years but have recently decided (with the encouragement and support of family) that it is okay to do things without him. I feel guilty leaving him behind. I worry about his safety when left with others. (Will they watch for every single thing like I do? What if he chokes? What if, what if, what if?) Not that I need validation from others, but I actually even worried about what other people think. "Can you believe they went on vacation and didn't even take Isaac?" Crazy, I know, but a parent's guilt and need to justify can be very strong.

So two years ago, Matt and I decided to take Charlie on a vacation to visit my sister in South Carolina. I agonized over the arrangements for Isaac and remember telling him a tearful goodbye and feeling like it was most likely the last time I would ever see him, as surely no one could take care of him like I do. Well, Isaac had a great time with his dad and various relatives while I was gone! He needs a vacation from me, and Charlie, Matt, and I need a vacation from him. I know that sounds callous, but it is most certainly true. It was good for all of us. It was a HUGE step for me to be separated from Isaac for a week. And just to make my ego feel better, the last night of our vacation, Isaac's dad phoned me to say, "Everything is okay, but we have Isaac in the emergency room."

He handled it well, but we ended up speeding up a little to get home to him! Sometimes, trying to include Isaac in everything our family does brings a great amount of stress to us. It took me seventeen years to be able to leave him, but I do believe it is beneficial for us to have some times of separation. It is good for Isaac and for the rest of us, and although I still feel tinges of guilt if I leave him, I know that it is okay, and he will be fine. And so will I.

Isaac and Jill

49

If you have seen Isaac in the last four years, then you have seen him holding beads in his hands. He must always have beads—Carnival/Mardi Gras beads! Why? Isaac has sensory processing issues, and in his particular case, he craves MORE sensory input which may be in the form of textures, sounds, sights, and tastes (maybe smells, but he doesn't provide reliable info). To give specific examples of how Isaac SEEKS extra sensory input: he likes flavorful food with extra taste, he wants fizzy/carbonated drinks, he wants spicy food, he wants music to be loud, he wants to hold hands/cuddle (which provides extra contact/pressure to his body), he constantly holds and rubs his beads (which gives him extra tactile input), he loves fireworks (the noise and the visual aspect), he LOVES lightning and thunder, and he wants to be barefoot (which allows him to FEEL temperatures and surfaces).

He craves the extremes. He loves to kick dirt/rocks so he can SEE dust clouds. He loves to hold his hot food up so he can SEE the steam. Isaac also tends to "chew" on his hands (maybe his mouth needs the sensation of more activity, or maybe he likes the sensation of the wet skin), and they are often calloused. He often makes loud noises so it gives him something to hear. He just wants EXTRA amounts of sensory input for all of his senses!

These issues were evaluated and addressed by his occupational therapist when he was in the 0–3 program, as well as Early Childhood programs. Isaac hasn't had any services from an occupational therapist since he was in second grade, which is an incredible negligence in my opinion. (The OT "couldn't work with" Isaac because he was silly and uncooperative, or maybe she was disorganized, unprepared, and not able to redirect him. Who knows?) Thankfully, Isaac's sister,

Lydia Reither Mathis, is now an OTR/L, and she is able to notice these sensitivities in Isaac and provide ways to try and help "level" his responses to sensations. Isaac won't get rid of these sensory issues, but with strategies, we can even him out and help him balance/regulate his input/responses!

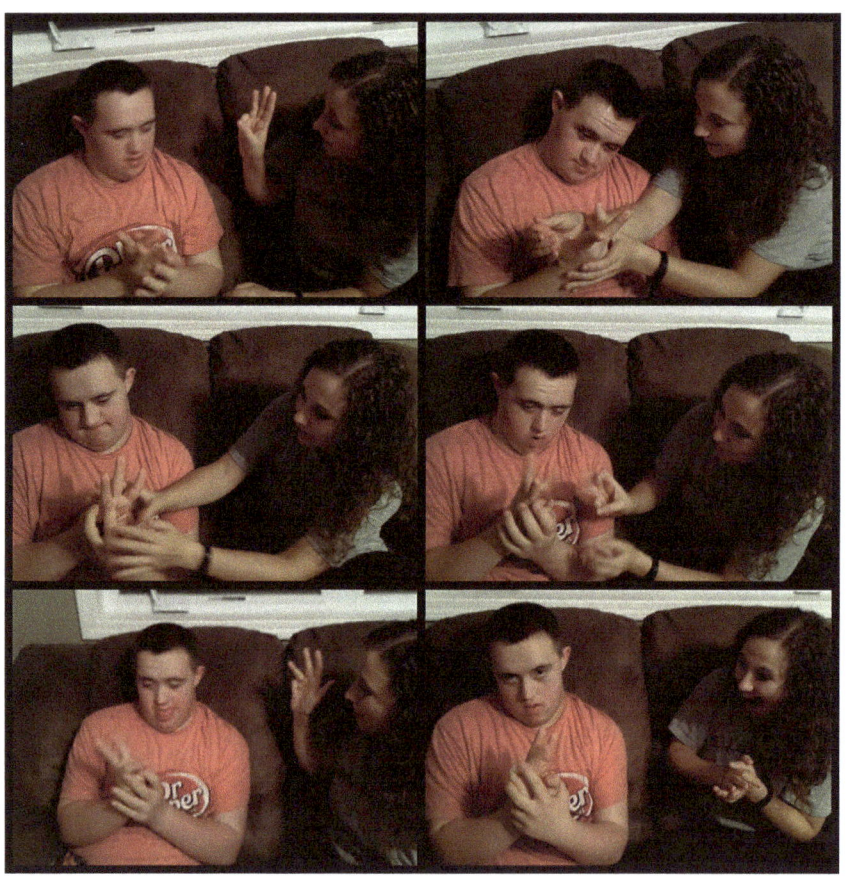

Isaac and his sister, Lydia, working on fine motor skills!

50

Down syndrome is the most commonly occurring chromosomal condition. Approximately one in every seven hundred babies in the United States is born with Down syndrome—about six thousand each year.

I've come across many articles about Down syndrome over the years, and I'm always eager to read them. Some of the recent articles I've read have titles such as these: "Thanks to Screening and Abortion We Are Headed toward a Down Syndrome Free World," "Down Syndrome Births Drop as More Women Abort," "Where Have All the Kids with Down Syndrome Gone?" "States Prohibit Abortion Based on Sex, Race, Genetic Abnormality," "Abortion after Prenatal Diagnosis of Down Syndrome Reduces Down syndrome Community by 30%," "As Soon as I Got the Prenatal Diagnosis I Knew What I Had to Do—End the Pregnancy," "In Iceland 100% of Babies with Down Syndrome Are Aborted," and "A World without Down Syndrome."

My opinion only: in my situation, it hasn't been about politics and rights. To me, it is just a sad commentary on humanity that we feel the need to eliminate any "defective" being. It doesn't seem like we are making progress as a society by eliminating people with Down Syndrome. I think if we use prenatal knowledge for preparation and education that it is beneficial to parents and medical providers. But my heart becomes very sad when I think of the possibility of a population that doesn't include people with Down syndrome.

Our society has made outstanding progress in the last few decades when it comes to providing medical care and education to people with Down Syndrome, learning about their abilities and realizing that these people can be positive, productive members of society. They have much to contribute. I've learned so many valuable life lessons from Isaac—strong patience, perseverance, finding joy in simple things, laughing at myself, the importance of serving others, slowing down to enjoy life, realizing it's okay to listen to Christmas music year-round, compassion, celebrating every day—the list goes on.

I'm not trying to judge others or condemn the decisions of others. I'm just speaking from my experience with Down syndrome. I've said it before: there are worse things than Down syndrome that DON'T show up on a prenatal test—a poor sense of humor, a superiority complex, a bully, poor taste in music (haha), etc.

After a routine blood test in my pregnancy with Isaac, my doctor told me I had a one in thirty-six chance of having a baby with Down syndrome and that baby has turned out to be one in a million to me!

51

The incidence of births of children with Down syndrome increases with the age of the mother. But due to higher fertility rates in younger women, 80 percent of children with Down syndrome are born to women under thirty-five years of age.

If I look at the charts that show a woman's chances of having a child with Down syndrome based on her age, a woman who is twenty-nine typically has about a one in one thousand chance of having a baby with Down syndrome. As a woman ages, the incidence of babies with Down syndrome increases so that around age forty, a woman has about a one in eighty-five chance of having a baby with Down syndrome. But because MORE younger women have babies, 80 percent of babies with Down syndrome are born to women under thirty-five.

That's how it was for me. I was twenty-nine when Isaac was born, then I was nearly forty-one when Charlie was born! I guess I'm a proof that young women can have babies with Down syndrome and also that older women can have babies without chromosomal abnormalities (glad I could be that scientific example for everyone!).

Although the statistics show that most babies with Down syndrome are born to women under thirty-five, I think it really catches these women by surprise. I know it caught me off guard. I remember NOT even thinking I needed to worry about Down syndrome because "that's usually for older women." When I was twenty-nine and knew my baby had Down syndrome, I remember sitting in waiting rooms with "older" pregnant women and feeling that it just really wasn't fair to me. Isn't it supposed to be those older ladies?

Fast forward twelve years later, I was forty (nearly forty-one) and pregnant again of all things! I was one of those "older" ladies now. I felt as though I was some freakish scientific anomaly—older (check), high risk (check), already have a child with Down syndrome (check), high blood pressure (check), gestational diabetes (check). We have a winner!

I was a pretty threatening presence at the doctor's office now. People made room for me—"Look out, here she comes." The worry was significant for a repeat pregnancy involving Down syndrome. And by significant, I mean more than you can imagine. I wasn't scared of having another baby with Down syndrome because I had a really good handle on what to expect. My worries were my age (because now I had the knowledge of what extra parenting needs would be required of me again), and Matt because I felt like he "deserved" a baby without a diagnosis. I didn't know if I would live long enough to provide another child with Down syndrome the care he needed for as long as he would need it, and I hated to think that Matt would have to care for a child with Down syndrome and wouldn't get to experience having a typical child.

I had many tests and sonograms with my pregnancy with Charles. I elected to not have any invasive procedures such as an amniocentesis, but I was encouraged to have (and did) a nuchal translucency scan, which searches for features which could indicate Down syndrome. During this scan, certain measurements were taken, one of the most important being the quantity of fluid collecting near the nape of the neck, which is a marker for Down syndrome.

This scan can also detect the cardiac abnormalities which are very common in Down syndrome. Everything looked "normal." I didn't really allow myself to believe that. I knew what the test results showed, but there is always room for errors. I kept it in the back of my mind that this baby might also have Down syndrome, and I wouldn't be convinced until he was born. And he was fine! So you see, a young mom can have a baby with Down syndrome, and an old mom can have a "normal" baby. It happens. It is all in God's grand plan.

52

Because Isaac has Down syndrome, our family is taking a different path. We listen to "The Chicken Dance" every day. We have learned to appreciate the simple things in life. We talk DAILY about our loved ones who have passed away. We have gained an awareness of people with differing abilities. We have learned that people with Down syndrome are individuals who are not "always happy" and always loving. We have Mardi Gras beads everywhere—house, cars, purse, etc. We have learned to "plan" for the unexpected. We have a routine. Every. Single. Day. We sort of feel like members of a club we didn't ask to join and certainly feel a kindred spirit with others in this "club." Our family has a child forever.

The extra chromosome Isaac possesses has brought great joy to our lives. It also brings great challenges which we try to embrace. Some days, it is easier than other days! God knitted Isaac together with this extra genetic material with such amazing and intriguing results! Proud to celebrate this extra chromosome! Proud to be part of the lucky few!

Isaac and Jill

53

For those who may not be aware of Isaac's beginnings, here's his "story":

I was twenty-eight years old when I became pregnant with Isaac. Although I already had five-year-old Lydia, I was naive when it came to medical testing. With my first pregnancy, I had all of the tests the doctor mentioned just because the doctor mentioned them! I hadn't ever given any thought to a test result that wasn't normal. I'd NEVER given it a thought! I just presumed that I'd have perfectly healthy, normal babies! Why wouldn't I? I was young and healthy!

After the triple screen blood test, the nurse phoned to say she was sure it was a false positive, but that my results indicated a strong possibility for a baby with Down syndrome. She said the doctor wanted me to have further testing, and I was scheduled for an amnio. Sure, okay. I'll be there!

I was working for my dad at the time, and I went down the hallway to his office, sat down, and started crying and told him what the nurse said. He was almost "irritated" at me for overreacting, I think! He said it was probably nothing and don't worry about it. Everything would be fine.

I think it was at that point that I just knew in my heart that the baby did indeed have Down syndrome. While waiting the week for the amnio, I outwardly tried convincing myself that everything WAS fine, that my baby didn't have Down syndrome, and that it was a false positive. But down in my heart and gut, I knew. And I knew that I had absolutely no knowledge about Down syndrome and what it meant for the baby, for me, for the rest of the family. I was even naive going into the amnio, asking what odds my blood test showed—one in thirty-six. Well, there's still a chance!

The doctor assured me that for my age, one in thirty-six was a significant chance. I had to know, so I had the amnio. Positive. Boy with Down syndrome. (In recent years, many use prenatal testing for "selection" purposes, which is NOT the point of this writing.) The very good thing about knowing ahead of time of this diagnosis was that the doctor was prepared. He was able to continually monitor for medical issues that he would otherwise not have been expecting. I was prepared. Our family was prepared. It is always a major undertaking to bring a baby into the world, but I cannot begin to imagine bringing a baby into the world without the "heads up" about a serious diagnosis.

Parents who receive a diagnosis at birth get the rug pulled out from underneath them. They are shocked. For my personality, that would not have gone well, and I'm ever so thankful that my naive or spacey self went through the prenatal tests so that Isaac could be monitored and his arrival could be planned and safe!

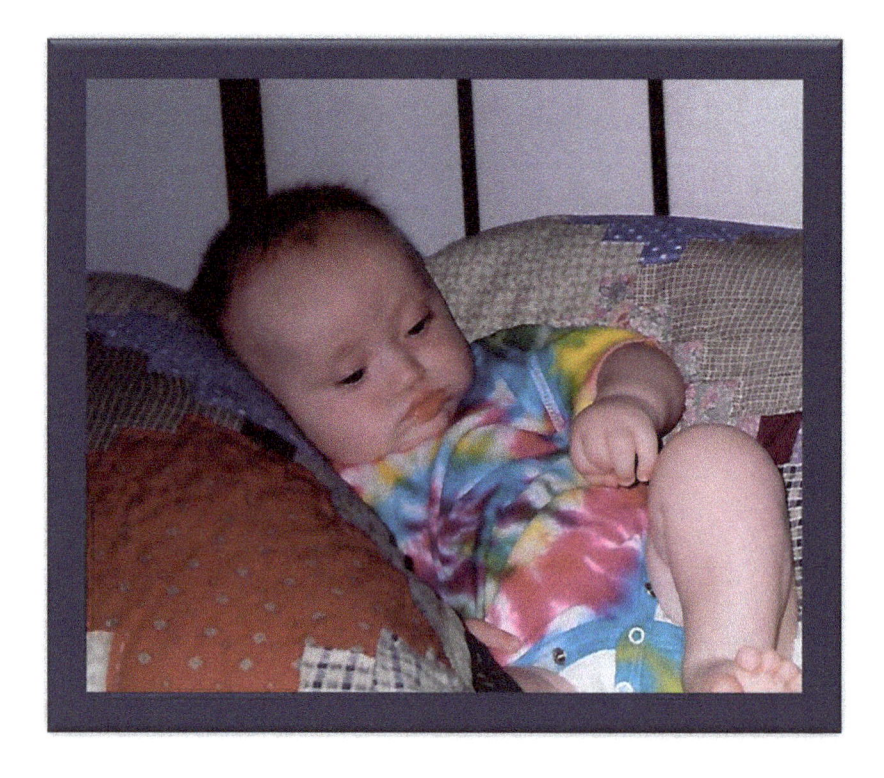

54

It is easy to love a baby! They are innocent, pure, snuggly, warm, they smell sweet. What's NOT to love about a baby? As a baby ages, he typically grows in size and maturity. It is what we expect. I have always had a particular love for babies, so I somehow feel God knew exactly His purpose in placing Isaac in my care. But when the "baby" reaches two hundred pounds and is often defiant, it is difficult to love every second!

Isaac still likes to snuggle (mostly with Matt, which Matt isn't always excited about doing with a two hundred-pound man!). We still cut up his food. He still cries when he gets upset. He still sucks his finger/hand when he's tired. We are still very active in bathing/toileting needs with Isaac. (Ya, he could do some of it on his own, but we want it done right! We want him to be clean! He doesn't need negative attention drawn to him for poor hygiene.) We still assist with dressing and shoes. So many aspects of Isaac's care are just like caring for a baby or toddler. His body grew, but his mind didn't.

As Isaac's siblings have aged, they have followed the typical physical and mental maturity (except I think Charlie has always been sixty-five years old). Sometimes it is challenging to "love" a two hundred-pound "baby," and to be honest, sometimes I'm a bit resentful that my baby didn't grow up like I would have expected him to do. He's a toddler stuck in a man's body and that isn't easy for any of us. I wonder what goes through his mind. Does he have internal struggles about the dichotomy of being nearly twenty years old in a man's body but with the mind of a toddler?

Does his mental ability allow thoughts like that? Does he feel "younger" than other twenty-year-olds? Does he understand that he isn't a typical twenty-year-old? His innocence and childlike characteristics are some of the qualities that endear him to me the most. Isaac may not always have the sweet smell of a baby or be the size of a toddler, but I really kind of enjoy it that he still likes to snuggle!

55

Communicating with Isaac has sometimes been challenging. As a baby and in his early years, he had regular speech therapy with the amazing Jan Ala, who with her skills and enthusiasm, was able to help our family actually communicate with Isaac! The early way was with sign language, and eventually one word or two.

As he learned to speak, he eventually dropped most of his signs, but signing was so valuable for him to be able to express to us what he could not verbally express. He has always had speech therapy through his school years, and it continues with the ever-patient Debbie Staton.

Over the years, Isaac's expressive verbal skills have continued to improve, but he still relies heavily on his family to "interpret" for him. For the most part, Isaac uses three- or four-word sentences. He is able to get his point across most of the time! But if you aren't used to being around Isaac, you will most likely have difficulty understanding him at first.

His speech intelligibility isn't always where we would like it! We have noticed recently that he is initiating more conversations with others though. He begins with a topic and then looks to one of us to relay his story. He may see someone and say, "Sad about Barkley," which is my cue to tell the listener that his dog recently passed away. Then he can answer questions or make a few comments about Barkley, but he has me tell the story!

Or he may say, "Pounds are bad," which I then relate that Isaac weighs too much but we are working on it! He loves to tell people his stories, usually the same ones repeatedly! He also often refers to himself as "Isaac," something like "Isaac wanna go there" or "Isaac do that."

As a family, we still applaud him when he uses complete sentences, even if it is something we don't want to hear! Over the summer, several times he would say, "I am hot!" And I would find myself saying, "Good talking, Isaac!" Even when I hear him say, "I am mad!" I can't help but compliment him on his speech! His comprehension of our language is excellent. He ALWAYS knows what we are talking about! Through his weekly speech therapy, his communication skills are still growing. We continue to see progress in how he is able to communicate with us!

Isaac with speech therapists Jan and Debbie,
and Early Childhood teacher, Becky

56

One of the highlights of Isaac's weeks is Sunday church. I'm not going to go so far as to say that he is a really religious guy, but he loves to go to church, and he truly does have the love of God in his heart! He loves the people there, the singing, the order of worship, and of course, the required trip to McDonald's afterwards (which the rest of the family isn't necessarily excited about).

He enjoys arriving at the church early each Sunday and visiting everyone, asking them what they had for supper, fibbing about what HE had for supper, telling them he's trying to cut down on soda, and listening to the choir warm up and practice.

Our director, Tim, is very patient with Isaac singing along during practice. I'm sure Isaac's singing doesn't "blend" well with the choir, but he is making his joyful noise to the Lord! During church, he looks forward to the singing of the hymns, hearing the announcements, the occasional mention of the name "Isaac" during a scripture reading (which always evokes an "ohhh!" when he hears his name), the choir singing, and even the Lord's Prayer (which he knows and says with congregation even though he is usually one to two words loudly behind).

He enjoys the sermon because that is when he either curls up next to Matt and lays his head on his shoulder or sneaks back a pew or two and sits with his friends, Chris & Brittney! Lately, Isaac has been helping his friend, Chris, collect the offering. You would think Isaac had been given the most important job in the world! He is so proud to be assisting with this and takes it so seriously.

The pride on that guy's face when he marches the offering up to the altar to give to "New Pastor" is priceless. Did I mention who New Pastor is? Our church welcomed a new minister and family nearly two years ago, and Isaac has referred to the pastor as "New Pastor" since then.

He greets him each week with a hearty "New Pastor!" I'm not sure at which point he will just become "pastor," but apparently, we haven't reached that time yet. And Isaac LOVES the final hymn, "Let There Be Peace on Earth," singing it with great gusto each week!

Isaac does have a couple of obstacles with church—any change in the order of worship and communion (because it changes the order of worship)! He likes it to be the same each week, no deviation!

On the way home from church, Isaac generally discusses who wasn't at church. He will say, "No La-La" or "No Gramma," listing whoever he DIDN'T see at the church. I usually try and make up an excuse for those who were absent—they were out of town, they may have been sick, etc. So just in case you ever think no one misses you when you're gone from church, you're wrong! Isaac always notices and wants to know where you are!

Isaac with several of his friends from church

57

As nice as it would be to think that Isaac is always happy (which is often a myth about people with Down syndrome), that isn't the case. I will say, that for the most part, Isaac's disposition is cheery. He is mostly jovial, always wanting others to be happy and laughing, and tends to share his good humor wherever he goes. That said, he is not ALWAYS happy. In fact, you may be surprised to know he gets quite angry.

The general public tends to think of people with Down syndrome in the following terms: loving, happy, mellow, sweet, quiet, childlike, complacent, easygoing. Sure, Isaac possess those qualities much of the time, but he is also completely capable of anger, disobedience, defiance, and a huge dose of stubbornness.

As Isaac has aged, we have noticed him exhibiting these qualities more frequently. But he is a teenager! What teenager doesn't exhibit those qualities? He is nineteen and basically micromanaged by someone twenty-four hours a day. It is completely normal for him to experience these emotions we aren't expecting from him!

What does Isaac get angry about? Sunny weather. He wants it to be rainy and cloudy. He loves rain and storms so that is what he wants. When he wakes up in the morning and the sun is shining, he addresses that issue first thing! "Hate it, sunny!" And he's upset. So we go through our "script" about how there is a chance of rain. "It may get cloudy later. Let's wait and see!"

We cannot watch the weather forecast at our house if Isaac is in the room. We cannot listen to the radio when they are broadcasting the weather. If there is any mention of sunny weather, Isaac gets angry. It generally takes quite a while to change his mood about this, and we are eager to point out ANY slight cloud in the sky to help him think it is cloudy!

Isaac also gets angry when told it is time for bed nearly EVERY night! How does he react? He yells, he says his "cuss" words, and he sometimes becomes somewhat pushy and aggressive.

We cannot avoid bedtime. It has to happen each night. We try setting a timer to give him a sense of how much time is left before bed. We try doing a countdown. We try a checklist of all the things that needed to be done before bed, and when they are all done, it's time for bed. Great strategies, but he sees through them!

We have recently discovered that if Matt and Charlie are in bed, I'm in my pajamas, the TV is off, the lights are off, and I go get in bed, he will EVENTUALLY walk down the hall to his room (but then I have to get up and get him situated and put his BiPAP on him). We don't feel too thrilled about leaving him alone in a room while everyone else is in bed, but this has been our most successful strategy so far!

The third thing that gets Isaac's anger emotions flowing is when he returns to my house after having spent a day or two with his dad! Environments are different, but he does not transition well. Again, he displays his displeasure by using his "cuss" words or yelling.

What are Isaac's cuss words? They are things he has come up with that he feels are hurtful, which he knows will evoke emotion from us. Words like fat, dead, died, naked, hate it, diarrhea. He uses these words in combination with whatever he is mad at: "Jill's fat, Jill died, sun's fat, hate it sun, Charlie diarrhea, phone's fat, phone's naked, etc." And the phone is mentioned because he does not like it when people are on the phone, particularly Matt! He wants Matt's attention. He does not want Matt giving attention to the phone!

There are other things that make Isaac angry, like a change in his schedule or situations that are unplanned/unexpected. The frustrating part is that we are unable to REASON with Isaac. We cannot make him understand that bedtime has to happen or that we have absolutely no control over the weather. He has the capacity to be upset over these things but does not possess the ability to be reasoned with on these things. We often feel like we are doing some lying to him by constantly telling him "it might rain later" or "it's supposed to get cloudy later," but it soothes his anger and makes the moment more pleasant for all of us! So if Isaac ever asks you if it's going to rain, be a sport and tell him, "Well, there's a chance!"

Isaac: All smiles on good days!

58

Isaac has designated a spot for himself in our living room. It is HIS spot, and he frowns upon it if anyone attempts to be in his area. This spot is on a love seat in a corner of our living room, a window behind him, and a window to his right. Upon arriving home from anywhere or finishing a meal or just waking in the morning, Isaac goes to his spot.

In this area, he keeps his "shrine" to those who have passed away (pictures in frames), his beads, his iPad, his headphones, Pig, his chargers, his talking toy parrot, his weather station, and a lighted color-changing ketchup bottle. He has everything he needs in his area! I believe he prefers this spot because he can see out the windows to watch for inclement weather, and he also has a full view of the entire living room so he can keep tabs on what everyone else is doing.

He will not sit on the other half of the love seat. He will not sit on the couch (unless he is going for a snuggle.) If we have guests and someone heads to his spot, he will anxiously stand by them and eventually point to another seat where he would like them to move. If there are other seats available in the living room, he prefers no one sit next to him.

Isaac is not interested in watching TV, so if others are watching, he sits in his spot and occupies himself with any one of his things. You can usually find him twirling his beads around, listening to "How Great Thou Art" (his favorite singers of this are Joey and Rory and Carrie Underwood), watching *Mr. Rogers* on YouTube while having his shrine set up next to him so he can have them listen, and talk to the shrine when he wants! (Yes, he talks frequently to those who have passed away.)

From his spot, he keeps the household up to date on what the temperature is and who has the corresponding number (63! Barney Stock!). I believe all of us have our spot where we feel most comfortable; however, Isaac is just more rigid in his willingness to try a different spot. He has found a place that works best for him and that is where he will always be!

59

Throughout Isaac's life, he has been entertained by very simple things. He has never truly enjoyed playing with toys (and it took our family several years to figure that out), but rather he is entertained by the effect of the toy (or object). These "likes" of his seem to have come in phases and the phases last for several years.

For a time (perhaps ages one to four years) he loved "slick ads." Yep, the colorful, slick advertisement pages that come with the newspaper, particularly a weekend edition. Isaac LOVED slick ads! He would sit with a pile of them and pick them up one at a time, hold over his head, release, and watch it float down. Cheap toy, you bet. This would occupy him for hours. He loved the feel of them, their texture, the way they floated, and we saved them so we would always have a pile of them.

Overlapping the "slick ad era" was the flour sack towel period. The plain flour sack towel was his constant companion. Don't try and decorate it, don't buy expensive ones, just plain white flour sack towels. For ten years, he received flour sack towels as gifts for Christmas and birthdays. He would wave the towel above his head as if it were a flag, fascinated with the way it would move. Sometimes he would wear it on his head, but mostly he waved it around. This era actually has mostly ended; however, he is often tempted to walk by one in the kitchen and pick it up.

Along with the towels, he has also always loved watching bedsheets be raised/lowered/fanned. He is mesmerized by that motion. Yet another phase he has been in is bubbles. He is still in this phase—heavily. We buy bubbles by the gallon, and he sits in the patio nearly year-round waving his bubble wand to create those enchanting bubbles that float through the air and sometimes blow to unexpected places. He LOVES bubbles. Again, it has to do with their motion.

SOMETHING EXTRA

Along this same line is his attraction to steam. He watches anything that is hot or steaming—my coffee, water in the shower, his soup or food, whatever is hot. If it is on his fork or spoon, he holds it up to eye level and watches the steam as long as he can, focusing on the motion of the steam.

I cannot recall HOW it began, but Isaac developed a love for Mardi Gras beads about seven or eight years ago. He has them with him all the time, and we have stashes of them in our cars, my purse, at the office, etc. Must. Have. Beads.

He also swings them around and rubs them. It is a soothing item for him, like the other items I've mentioned. (In a crisis of no beads one time, his dad gave him a rosary, and he would not use it because it is not a solid strand of uniform beads.)

All of these items he has loved show his need for sensory stimulation. He requires a lot of sensory input. These examples have been mostly visual or textural, and they help him feel order in his life.

60

Isaac graduated from Triopia High School in May. Our goal is to have him attend an area day training program, but due to lack of state funding, he has returned to Triopia. Isaac is sort of "done" with school, so at his IEP, we tried to develop some tasks that could give him some life skills and keep him interested in something.

In the past few years, Isaac has done vacuuming at school, assisted in the cafeteria, and also sorted mail. This year, his new role is a coffee service. He purchased a Keurig, cups, lids, coffee and tea pods, sugars and creamers, etc., with his own money. The school developed a Google form that is distributed to staff and set up an email address for Isaac which he must log in to each day and check his coffee orders.

His aide, Tara, helps him, and they line up their cups for the day and keep track of when the beverages need to be made and delivered. The teachers may purchase punch cards from Isaac, so he also has to handle money (and he also punches the cards, which is a great fine motor activity!).

Tara assists Isaac in making the drinks, and he has learned which buttons to push and how to operate the Keurig. (Bonus for Isaac is that he gets to sit and watch the steam as the beverage heats!)

I have always felt one of Isaac's greatest strengths is his "people skills," so I have a feeling that he especially enjoys delivering the beverages and socializing with the teachers/staff. Just when I think Isaac has plateaued in his learning, I'm happily surprised he has a new skill set! This coffee endeavor has given Isaac a real purpose, given him new skills, given him the opportunity to have responsibilities, and provided him with interaction with "customers."

SOMETHING EXTRA

He won't get rich at this project, he's just trying to break even! He has days where he makes and delivers five drinks and days when it is ten or twelve drinks.

Another unplanned benefit of this project is that Isaac is moving more and getting more physical activity by walking through all parts of the building delivering his drinks. He may become bored with this project at some point in time, but for now, it is great for him! Our family has always been thankful for the willingness of our school district and staff to find ways to keep Isaac engaged in learning!

61

Isaac loves holidays. His natural wonder and excitement of holiday traditions makes it even more enjoyable for the rest of us. He still goes trick or treating dressed as a hot dog. That has been his costume for the last nine years. It works for him. He loves trudging around Arenzville, at least three houses behind Charlie, knocking on doors and collecting his treats. Maybe he just loves it because it is an opportunity to see people.

Since Isaac has an eight-year-old brother, it has been easy to continue taking Isaac trick or treating. I imagine I'll still take Isaac door-to-door even when Charlie's enthusiasm has faded.

Last week, Charlie and I were discussing costume possibilities, and Isaac announced, "Isaac be a hot dog! Oh, boy!"

When it comes to Easter, Isaac still enjoys a good egg hunt! He delights in searching the house and yard for the treasure to be found in plastic eggs. I've taken him to the local hunt a couple of times with Charlie. The first year I tried to just let it be for Charlie, but Isaac didn't understand and wanted his own basket. He wants to hunt eggs. Of course, what sixteen-year-old doesn't? He was in the older children's category.

As they started hunting, the other children raced around grabbing eggs while Isaac plugged along, occasionally bending over to pick up an egg before it was snatched up by a quicker hunter! I have a feeling he'll still be wanting to hunt eggs for many more years.

Although Isaac knows that Christmas is the time our family celebrates the birth of Jesus, his mind is full of excitement about Santa! He still enjoys going to see Santa and sitting on his lap (not sure Santa likes this, considering Isaac's "pounds are bad"!). Isaac usually tells Santa that he wants soda and ketchup, of course. And Isaac

LOVES Christmas songs, listening to them and singing along makes him so happy!

The last few years he has enjoyed a trip on the Polar Express or similar train, and he is downright giddy when Santa makes his appearance! So wide-eyed and happy!

For now, Charlie is still a believer, but it won't last. I envision Isaac will keep this enthusiasm for the rest of his life. He will always make the holidays a sweeter time because he has such innocence and wonder, and didn't we all have that when we were younger? I'm thankful (and a little jealous) that Isaac has the ability to see life like this.

JILL ROEGGE

62

Something that I never really noticed about Isaac until the last few years is his ability to make other people truly happy. When he was growing up, I felt like people were always polite around him, accepted him (for the most part), and genuinely cared about him, but I hadn't realized that he makes people happy just by being Isaac. I don't always notice this at the time when he is with people, but later I notice it if a photo has been taken and I see the expressions on others faces. It is usually a candid picture where I notice it—nothing posed, just genuine smiles.

Sometimes Isaac isn't even actually smiling, but he has said or done something that has brought genuine happiness to those around him. The neat thing about that is that he doesn't even know he's bringing happiness. He's innocent to it. He's not trying. He's just being Isaac. There is something pure about his ways. His spirit is contagious. He is uninhibited, and I think we enjoy seeing that in people. We often see that unrestrained emotion and unabashed zest for life in children, but as we age, we lose that. We become self-conscious, guarded, and hold back. Isaac never lost that, and he lives spontaneously, carefree, and in the moment.

Somewhere in that extra chromosome is a segment that holds a key to happiness, an enthusiasm for life, a way of living life without worry of what others think of you, living and treating others with honesty—no ulterior motive. Again, I'm jealous of the way Isaac is able to live like this. His life has certainly been blessed by God.

63

Isaac was eleven when Charlie was born. Now their ages are nineteen and eight. Some days are great between these two—laughing, sharing, helping. Some days are pretty tense between these two. As mature as Charlie is for an eight-year-old, sometimes it wears him down to be around Isaac. Isaac teases him quite frequently. He tells everyone he sees about things Charlie does, even embarrassing things. Isaac's need for routine often dictates our family's activities, which can sometimes disrupt Charlie's expectations or plans. I still have hope that their relationship will strengthen positively as Charlie ages. I did an impromptu interview with Charlie last night and these were his responses.

"What is it like to have a brother with Down syndrome?" I asked.

"Sometimes it's fun and sometimes it's frustrating," Charlie answered.

"How is it fun?"

"When he says stuff that is funny! Like when he sings, 'Kum ba yah' and changes the words to things like, 'Someone's tired, Lord, kum ba yah' or 'Someone's hungry, Lord, kum ba yah.'"

"How is it frustrating?"

"When he says, 'chick, chick Charlie' and calls me names. It's kind of annoying that he listens to the same songs over and over all the time. And I think that I get in trouble more than Isaac and that's not fair. He gets away with more stuff. Sometimes I have to help a lot more because he can't do things for himself."

"What do you like best about Isaac?"

"That he can play sports. He's pretty happy. It makes me feel good that he talks about Grampa and Gramma Roegge a lot because he knows I miss them and that means he misses them too. I think he talks about them because he's trying to make me feel better and let me know he hasn't forgotten them."

"Do you ever feel sad that Isaac has Down syndrome?"

"Not really."

"Does he ever embarrass you?"

"Yes. When he tells people things that happened at home like when I was sick at Christmas last year and he still keeps telling everyone I had diarrhea. That's embarrassing."

"Do you ever wish he didn't have Down syndrome?"

"Sometimes. But it's okay that he has it."

"How do you think he would be different?"

"He'd be like Wade. He'd like to play with me. He would do stuff with me that a normal brother would. He'd probably play baseball with me. He could drive me anywhere. I bet he would help out on the farm."

"Do you think you learn anything from Isaac?"

"It is different than having a normal brother. I have to wait on him a lot. He takes a longer time to get ready. He's older than me, but I think I am the one that helps him. Usually it's the older brother that helps the younger one."

64

Isaac's life is very orderly. He likes it that way. No, he REQUIRES it that way! He doesn't like "stuff" and has very few possessions. He always has the tidiest room in the house. He never makes messes—never has! He doesn't care about "things," but if things are around, he prefers them neat and in order.

The nontangible aspects of Isaac's life are also neat and orderly—his routines, his schedules, his activities. He awakes in the morning with a robust, "Good Morning! It's Tuesday!" Sometimes he says "Tuesday is starting!" and we're off and running! He may not have an internal clock, but he was most definitely blessed with a never failing internal calendar, as he ALWAYS knows what day of the week it is.

Once awake and the day has been announced, he swipes his beads off his dresser, shuts his door and trudges to the kitchen to await his customary three scrambled eggs drizzled with ketchup, cup of sugar-free chocolate pudding, glass of chocolate milk, and his daily meds.

Of course, his meal is consumed in the same way each day, and upon completing each item, he announces "ta-da, ta-da!" Then he heads back down the hall for his shower. Must weigh in first, announce pounds, go potty, reweigh, announce pounds again. Await shower to warm up (while gazing in mirror and making silly faces and laughing).

Once in the shower, he hands me (or Matt) the shampoo, and we shampoo his hair. While rinsing, he ritualistically squeals "ooo-hhheee!" Hands me the soap to pour on his bath scrubby and away he goes washing. His showering routine involves him counting and pouring cups of water over his head. He likes to get to at least nineteen cups, his age. Sometimes it is fewer, and sometimes it is way more than nineteen, depending on what I'm trying to accomplish in the rest of the circus tents.

Next we do the drying routine which begins with eleven steps in place and then the body drying wherein he says "seven arms," and I say "one arm" and dry the first arm. He laughs and says, "eight arms," and I say "two arms" and dry the second arm.

Then "nine legs," and I say "one leg" and dry the first leg. He laughs and says, "ten legs," and I say "two legs" and dry the second leg.

Each of the lines in this script he has established are very important to him. Must complete all steps before moving to next step. And we continue getting ready, following more scripts and actions just so we can end up dressed and ready to go out the door. Do we all like these scripts and routines? Heck, no. But if we follow them, our mornings are much more pleasant. Isaac thrives in these systematic ways. He loves knowing what will be happening "later," what we will be eating for supper, and if it will be raining. I do my best to give him an answer that will satisfy him, but must admit I'm not always honest with him. Sometimes because I truly don't know the answer, and sometimes my dishonesty is for his own benefit to avert a meltdown from him.

Change is not always welcome. He makes it through his school day and when I pick him up each day, we have a familiar script we follow. And as we exit the school parking lot, he exclaims, "Tuesday is over!"

I always smile to myself when he announces the day is over! It is almost like someone just made a red *X* through the day in his mental calendar! His days are orderly and neat. He wouldn't have it any other way! And guess what? "Wednesday is starting!"

SOMETHING EXTRA

65

Not everyone with Down syndrome possesses the same qualities that I have described in my writings. Everyone is unique with their own set of individual characteristics like any person. Isaac tends to be very social, generally happy, childlike, lower functioning academically, speaks in more broken sentences, quite behind in maturity for someone his age.

There are many people with Down syndrome who are very high functioning and able to participate in regular education programs, college courses, live independently, have a mature relationship with someone and perhaps even marry, and be gainfully employed. (I've seen the TV shows a time or two, but I don't watch them.)

For our situation, that isn't realistic. Although Isaac is teachable and has many skills, he realistically is not at that higher level. And that's fine, it is WHO Isaac is. Does it bother me? Sometimes it does. Sometimes I wish he was capable of more, able to do more things, function higher, be able to have more meaningful conversations, be able to reason with him. But I accept him for who he is and what he can do, trying not to think of what he isn't able to do.

When I have seen the reality shows featuring people with Down syndrome, I do tend to become a bit cynical, feeling like they are featuring only the more higher functioning folks and giving the public the misconception that ALL people with Down syndrome are that high functioning.

People with Down syndrome are all different, with different abilities, strengths, and weaknesses. When Isaac was born, my dad (who was known for his wit) made the statement that if Isaac was "mildly affected" by Down syndrome, he could be a real estate appraiser. And if he was "severely affected," he could be a lawyer. The verdict is still pending!

Isaac and his classmates from the Triopia
High School Class of 2018

66

Many people use the term or phrases about OCD in a casual way. "Man, my OCD is really acting up" or "I'm so OCD about ____." And people are often picky about details, no doubt about it. But to actually have obsessive-compulsive disorder truly takes things to a different level.

Isaac is both obsessive and compulsive. Our family is used to the things he is obsessive about, so we probably don't "notice" it so much anymore. I tried to pay particular attention to him this week and observe when he became unable to move forward or unable to complete a task. I snapped a few pictures when I would think about it. He has difficulty if he sees a cabinet door left open or slightly ajar. He will stop what he is doing, get up from a meal, or walk across a room to close it, then resume his activity.

He was eating breakfast at our table, looked over and saw an ink pen clicked down and had to get up, walk across the room, click the pen, then was able to finish eating. Same situation when he saw a ketchup bottle with the lid open—must get it closed. He walks around the house closing lids, clicking pens, shutting doors and drawers.

If the shower curtain is slightly ajar, it must be fixed; a hand towel hanging unevenly is sure to cause him stress. Upon entering the shower, he will close any lids that previous shower takers have left open, and an open toothpaste lid cannot be ignored.

Granted, I would probably react the same way and close lids or doors, but the difference is that he cannot proceed. I could let it go for a while, not that I'm being slobby or lazy, but that it doesn't paralyze me.

SOMETHING EXTRA

It is very real to him. These things MUST be fixed. They need to be in order, and if not, it is very disruptive to him.

Similar to this is his need for repetition. The way he settles on a number and then must listen to a song that many times. For instance, if his chosen number for the day is eleven, he is insistent on listening to his songs eleven times each, watching his videos eleven times, etc. His repetitive habits are very soothing to him, part of his order, and closing doors, drawers and lids makes him feel comfortable, just like we all have things that make us feel things are right with the world!

67

Isaac is not interested in TV. The following shows are an exhaustive list of what he WILL watch: *Mr. Rogers* (his favorite), *Barney* (the dinosaur), *The Wiggles, America's Funniest Videos* (which he calls "Funny Stooges"), *Sesame Street,* and *Teletubbies.*

We think of young children as watching cartoons, but I think Isaac cannot relate to the animation. It is too busy and abstract for him. He prefers the listed shows because they have real people in them. Most of these shows are not on TV anymore, but thankfully, he has figured out YouTube and is able to watch these videos and not always in English!

He is very proficient using the iPad and can find his channel and watch his shows. Keep in mind he has been watching these same episodes for more than fifteen years, and he has them memorized. He has the scripts memorized, the music memorized, and he could masterfully be an understudy for ANY cast member of these episodes. He knows all of the acting, hand movements, facial expressions, etc. He's got it!

Some of my favorite times with Isaac are when he's watching *Mr. Rogers* and singing along with songs from *Mr. Rogers,* the "Creation Duet" or "Then Your Heart is Full of Love." He prefers the gentleness and calm found in the "beautiful neighborhood of make believe."

He enjoys watching *America's Funniest Videos* with others around him mostly because I think he enjoys seeing people laugh. I'm not even sure he is watching the show, but rather he's watching for other people's reactions. He loves to watch people laugh!

When our family is gathered and watching TV, Isaac is always present, but he doesn't pay attention to it unless he sees someone on the screen who is exhibiting sadness or there is emotional tension, then he requests we change the channel. He is not a fan of anything that would appear sad or scary. He loves the positive shows filled with music and make believe!

68

Isaac's siblings are, perhaps, the most important relationship he has. Aaron, Lydia, and Charlie have either been with him since HIS first day or THEIR first day! These people have watched him grow, develop, learn to walk, learn to talk, and reach other milestones. And they have loved him and been proud of him. They have also witnessed him struggle to learn things, attempt and fail things, exhibit embarrassing behavior in public, have meltdowns in public, and seen him be stared at in public. And they have loved him and been proud of him. They have been his biggest cheerleaders despite the sometimes embarrassing situations he can cause. They have stood up for him, constantly corrected people who use the *R* word. They have advocated for him and others similar to him. They have proudly taken him on dates, to ball games, and to concerts, and included him.

I am a parent of someone with differing abilities. I am not a sibling. I don't have ANY experience as a sibling to someone like Isaac. I can't speak for them, but I know it hasn't always been easy. It has sometimes been embarrassing. It has been stressful. It has meant they had to be more patient. It has meant they often had to take less attention from their parents because we were busy with Isaac and his needs. That's reality.

As a parent, I feel guilty about the discrepancy of distribution of attention that happened. I couldn't help it. It was how our family had to function. Fortunately for Isaac, his siblings have been and continue to be absolute champion siblings. He has been blessed beyond measure with compassionate, patient, understanding, accepting, encouraging, giving, helpful siblings. His presence has enriched and influenced their lives, helping to shape who they are and how they interact with others.

SOMETHING EXTRA

69

Isaac calls me "Jill." He has always referred to me that way. He also calls me "Poppy," and we aren't certain where that originated. Sometimes he even calls me "Poppy Jill," but rarely "Mom." He has grown up hearing Lydia call me Mom, and he has heard Charlie call me Mom for many years now, but he chooses to call me Jill.

I have always wanted him to call me Mom, but after nineteen years, I'm resigning myself to be called Jill. The exception for him calling me Mom is when he is sick, sad, or worried. Then I'm Mom, Mommy, or Mama Jill. When he is sad and crying about his dog, Barkley, he comes to me crying "Mommy!" When he doesn't feel well, he calls me Mommy. Yesterday he was very worried about my bandaged hands and hugged me so tightly crying, "Oh, Mommy! Sorry about arms!"

It is somehow comforting to me to know that in his worst times, when he is feeling his lowest, he knows he needs his mom, such a natural response for most of us.

70

When Isaac was three, I learned something about him, and I've thought about it nearly every day for the last sixteen years. Isaac started early childhood classes in Beardstown (a ten-mile distance from our house) a few days after his third birthday.

He was not too verbal at this age. He was going to be riding the bus from our home to his classes each day, on a school bus, with people he didn't know, to an unfamiliar place. I was so worried about his reactions and fears, thinking he would have NO IDEA where he was going, why he was going, what he would be doing, when he would return, etc.

I decided I would ride the bus with him the first day and talk to him throughout the ride, explaining what was happening and reassuring him. Know what? He did not care one bit that I was in that bus with him. He was fine! He was excited! This is what I learned: he lives IN the moment, not worrying about the next. He didn't worry about where he was going, who would be there, what he would do when he got there—he just went. He trusted.

Every night he goes to bed and I wonder what he thinks because he certainly doesn't express any anxiety over the upcoming day (other than what he will eat and if it will rain!). Every morning, he greets the day with a hearty pronouncement of the day, excited that a new day has even arrived, not really expecting that a new day would arrive but happy that it did. He is appreciative of each new day. He has no preconceived notions about what the day will be like. It will be what it is. What a sweet gift God has bestowed on Isaac—no worries for what the day holds, no stresses. I'm quite envious of this trait in Isaac's personality. Wish I could be more like him!

JILL ROEGGE

Isaac and Daddy Matt

71

As any parent does, I try and make plans for my children's well-being and care if something should happen to me. It isn't something anyone really wants to plan, but it is a necessity. A child with a disability "obligates" a parent in a little different way than a typical child.

Most of us never actually think other arrangements will be necessary. We think "my child will grow up before I pass away" or "my child can go live with Aunt _____ if something ever happens to me,"—always knowing these arrangements won't ever become a reality. But it is a real possibility that Isaac could outlive me. He isn't able to live on his own. He doesn't have the skills needed to take care of himself. It is not like I would be leaving a cute little toddler who will grow up and leave the nest at around age twenty-two (what typical parents plan for).

Isaac will be a time-consuming, attention-demanding, potentially costly, permanent inheritance for someone. I think that is why I have delayed my future planning as long as I have. I've struggled with this situation throughout Isaac's life, never wanting to face the possibility that I could be "leaving him" in the care of someone else.

How do you ask someone to take over the care of a child who comes with many not-so-fun strings attached? Will Isaac be happy living with this person? Will this person grow weary of caring for Isaac? Will Isaac be looked after and provided with all he needs? Of course, no one else can take care of him like I do! Ha!

Over the years I have jotted down instructions about Isaac's care, listed his meds, made certain others knew his routines, and made certain others knew what I really wanted for his future. When Isaac turned eighteen, I obtained legal guardianship of him, as he cannot responsibly make legal decisions. But it wasn't until this year that I finally took the plunge and worked with an attorney to set up Isaac's future care and special needs trust. I had decided that the chances of the most perfect scenario (Isaac and I passing simultaneously) probably wasn't realistic. This was a process I had avoided mostly because it forced me to think of my own mortality and also because I have never wanted to burden anyone with caring for Isaac. It's asking a lot of someone! I have a sense of relief now knowing that plans are in place should they be needed. It isn't something that parents want to think about doing, but I believe that if we want what is best for our children, we should legally makes these plans.

Isaac is always surrounded by people who are protective of him: cousins, grandparents, siblings, and friends

72

Although Isaac is nineteen, he doesn't have much of a concept of safety or what to do in an emergency. I admit it: we hover over him. But we do it for his own protection. He has not proven to us that he knows how to react if there would happen to be an emergency.

A few years ago, his dad had a fall on the ice and was unconscious on the pavement. Isaac left him and walked into a gas station to get a drink and look around. When asked by employees where his dad was, Isaac responded "fell." It didn't enter his brain that this was a situation that needed help. (It was after this incident that we outfitted Isaac with an ID bracelet when we go out in public.)

Isaac doesn't realize that walking into a street is a hazard. He rarely looks for oncoming cars before crossing a street. When we are in parking lots, he always reaches for my hand, though, showing that he is somewhat aware there could be danger. When we are at home, I sometimes go outside for a few minutes, leaving him unattended in the house, and I worry about him!

Usually the worst thing he does if left unattended is get a soda or a snack! But there are so many potential everyday hazards that could hurt him. He could try and use the microwave. He could try and use the gas stove. He could cut himself if he tried cutting anything. He could use electricity too close to water. He could fall down steps, etc. He doesn't KNOW that these things could harm him; hence, the hovering.

We cannot leave him unattended. Even Charlie has realized that Isaac could be in danger if left alone, and he has become a great protector and helper when needed. The last three summers I have had Charlie keep an eye on Isaac while I mow our yard, and I stop every fifteen minutes or so and check on them. Charlie knows to flag me down if he needs assistance. I typically have them outside blowing bubbles and within sight. I often think that if he and I were together and I had an emergency, he would not know how to react. I have always straddled the fence on whether talking to him about emergencies and teaching him about 911 is a good idea. Would he call it at inappropriate times or would he not even consider calling it? Would talking about emergency situations scare him, make him worry, or even affect him? We want Isaac to be safe. We try and give a cautious amount of independence to Isaac but keep a realistic eye on him.

Charlie leading Isaac out to check on calves

73

As I've said before, each person with Down syndrome is an individual with differing presentations of Down syndrome. Sometimes the presence of the extra twenty-first chromosome shows itself mildly, other times more so.

Just like the typical population, no two people are the same. Isaac happens to have a quite low IQ, but he makes up for it in charm and personality! He may be on the autism spectrum and have a hefty case of OCD, but he has a great sense of humor and makes us laugh!

Is it easy to parent Isaac? Heck, no! Is it easy to parent any child? Heck, no! It is just different. I'm doing care for my nineteen-year-old that typical parents quit doing around age four for their typical kids. But in "exchange," I have experienced a pretty charmed teenage season with Isaac. No worries about him driving, socializing inappropriately, staying out too late.

Some days it takes all my strength to be patient with Isaac. Some days I need lots of help with him. It often does take the village to help with him. There are days that I truly wish Isaac DIDN'T have Down syndrome, not for my benefit, but for his. There are many things in life I wish he could experience—that he never will. That stings my heart.

And on the flip side, there are many things he experiences that make me jealous—his sense of wonder at lightning, his reaction to popcorn popping, his no-stress life, awesome!

Recently Charlie said, "I'm not saying Isaac shouldn't have Down syndrome, but if he didn't, I bet he'd be farming and driving me around."

Ya, I sometimes allow myself to drift there, to the "what if" dreams. Admittedly, our family is stressed with Isaac many times, but I believe God is rewarding ME by allowing me to be Isaac's mom (I sometimes need reminded of this!). I believe God will continue to bless our family and allow us to see the silver lining in this extra chromosome. We have learned compassion, the necessity of humor, humility, simplicity, love, the importance of slowing down, acceptance, the importance of advocacy, and oh, so many more life lessons from Isaac. He is an amazing teacher, and I'm proud to call him my son.

74

Isaac ENJOYS doing the weekly grocery/Walmart shopping. Why? Because it is a social outing for him! When Isaac goes along with me, I can pretty much at least DOUBLE the time I spend in a store. That's because so many people stop and visit with him! He loves it! He seems to know more people than I do. And if he sees someone at the end of an aisle who he knows, we can't just walk on by. Nope, he often trots clear down an aisle to make contact with someone he knows from church or school. He visits with all the clerks he can! And they are always happy to interact with him. It's sort of like travelling with a rock star (that's how our friends Jeff and Cheryl Baer describe it when they take their son, Phillip, on errands!). We can't go anywhere without someone (usually several people) coming over and talking to Isaac, and it brightens his day, and our family appreciates it!

75

Isaac will turn seventeen in December. Charlie turned five in June. There is sort of a role reversal going on in our house—younger brother behaving more like an older brother. Although Charlie is younger, he is already beginning to be protective of Isaac and assist him with tasks. He takes Isaac's hand when we're in a parking lot or store to HELP Isaac, not because he's the five-year-old who should be holding a hand!

Charlie knows Isaac has Down syndrome, and he's asked when Isaac was going to be done with Down syndrome. Charlie is somewhat understanding of Isaac's unique way of doing things but hasn't quite reached the level of maturity where he can completely tolerate Isaac's idiosyncrasies and ignore his repetitive/ritualistic tendencies, but he's getting there!

Being the sibling of any child with a diagnosis is a challenge. It's downright tough sometimes. Charlie and I recently watched the movie *Where Hope Grows*, and he completely identified the main character who had Down syndrome with Isaac. In fact, at particularly sensitive part of the movie, he began weeping (and continued for at least ten minutes) because he was substituting Isaac in to the circumstances of the movie, saying, "I don't want this to happen to Isaac."

He is young, but he is "getting" what Down syndrome is about and the impact it has on our family All of Isaac's siblings have gained a greater level of patience, compassion, empathy, and level of awareness of people with disabilities. Even though it may have been challenging for them, these qualities will be valuable assets to them for the rest of their lives.

SOMETHING EXTRA

Isaac and Charlie

76

I know it is sometimes difficult to try and have a conversation with Isaac. Here are a few hopefully "helpful" insights when you're talking with him. Isaac does not like silence or lulls in conversations. If this happens, he will begin saying random words (which he is expecting me to explain to you), making noises or start with one of his "scripts." His scripts are his "material," talking about his dad's accident, telling you his sister has a big test, telling you words he's not supposed to say, etc. He will begin to dominate the conversation with nonsense words/phrases.

To avoid silences, just have a "normal" conversation around him. He is smart enough to chime in with appropriate comments but reverts to silly ones to get a laugh. Isaac typically uses just a few words per sentence and then relies on someone in his family to "interpret" what he is telling you. We try and encourage him to use complete sentences but that just doesn't happen. There are many times when Isaac has extreme difficulty in getting the first parts of words out and it is a lengthy "stutter," and when this happens, we just try and be patient and wait for him to get the word out. He's really trying but can't get past the first sound in the word!

And if you want to have a conversation with Isaac that interests him, here's are some ideas: the weather (think it will rain? Has it been windy? Cloudy? Warm? Cold?), ask about his dogs, Barkley and Max (have they been chasing each other in the yard? Barking a lot?), or anything about food (have you been out to eat lately?)

He will often want to tell you words he's not supposed to say. They aren't necessarily bad words, but they are words that have caused trouble for him, or he's been so repetitious with them that we are trying to get him to stop saying them, i.e., "chick-chick" and "juicy."

SOMETHING EXTRA

Isaac also likes to put the word "somebody" after MANY words he says. For example, "Chocolate milk, somebody?" "Thunderstorm, somebody?" It's not always easy to talk with him, I know, and I always appreciate everyone's attempts and patience with him!

Isaac and Jill before a t-ball game

77

Isaac doesn't really have any concept of time. He can usually look at a clock and tell us what time it is, but it basically means very little to him. For instance, if I say, "We're going to need to leave in about an hour," that means absolutely nothing to him! The only "times" that he is interested in are "time to eat" and "time for bed." The rest of the hours in a day don't concern him.

He's very insistent on getting his pajamas on as soon as it becomes dark, but he wouldn't know or care what time it was. (And with the upcoming time change, yes, he will be asking for pajamas around 6 p.m.)

When Isaac wakes up, he's ready to get up and that can also be during the middle of the night. Many times he has awakened during the night and just gets up. He's been known to get out of bed during the night, go to the kitchen, have snacks and turn all the lights on in the house, play his iPad and have sort of an "Isaac party." He doesn't realize that it's the middle of the night. We still use a "baby" monitor so we can tell if he's getting up during the night. I'm a hostage to a clock, always trying to get somewhere by a certain time, get things done on time, make time for this/that. I'd rather be a little more like Isaac.

SOMETHING EXTRA

78

Isaac used to choke frequently when he was younger, most likely attributed to his lack of chewing. On one occasion, the first responders/fire department were called because we were unable to get his choking resolved. He hasn't forgotten that day.

Isaac pretty much knows what foods will give him difficulty, and he's good about refusing those foods. At home, he refuses foods with nuts, suckers, grapes, hard candies, and he will often remind us he has "trouble with the pork"! (And he does have trouble with pork, different texture. He does best with ground meat.) He doesn't allow himself to have those foods because he knows they are choking hazards.

In the last couple of years he has allowed himself to get cough drops at school, although that may just be a ploy to get out of class and visit with the office secretary! It's not always a pleasant visual dining experience to eat with Isaac. He likes to have ketchup on most things, which is a turnoff to others, but he will eat most foods if even a few drops of ketchup is put on! And he tends to do lots of "lip-smacking" while he's eating, which can be an annoying noise to other diners.

When Isaac eats a plate of food, he finishes one item completely before moving on to the next one. And after each portion is consumed, he proudly announces the item and says, "Corn! Ta-Da! Ta-Da!" or "Meatloaf! Ta-Da! Ta-Da!" He then expects us to compliment him on each finished item!

SOMETHING EXTRA

79

Many times people with Down syndrome get labeled as always being happy. Well, these people are human and not ALWAYS happy! Isaac gets upset/emotional about several things. He misses his sister, he gets mad when Charlie wants the iPad, and he gets mad when I tell him he can't have more food or when his routine gets changed. And sometimes he is upset or feeling anxious, and we don't know the cause.

There are two things that Isaac does that indicate that he's feeling anxious—he makes "the face" or he begins rubbing/pulling out his hair in the front of his head. "The face" is sort of a look of disgust, recognizable by those of us close to him. When we see it, we know something is bothering him. We all try and figure out what's wrong because he's "making the face"! The hair pulling comes and goes.

He may be obsessed with his hair for two months at a time and pull lots of it out or he may go six months and completely leave it alone. But when he's pulling his hair, it is usually a sign of some anxiety. During certain times of the year, we can tell how Isaac's day has been based on how his hair looks! He doesn't know how to hide these things. For me and probably many other typical folks, when we are anxious or stressed we try and hide it so others won't know. Once again, Isaac is genuine.

SOMETHING EXTRA

Isaac is happiest when surrounded by friends and family

80

Isaac provides VERY little information about what goes on during his school day.

"How was school today?"

"Fine."

"What did you have for lunch?"

"Chicken."

"What did you do in PE?"

"Football. Hate it."

And then he's done talking about school. If I ask more questions I get this: "Jill, stop it."

Historically, Isaac's answers aren't "reliable" either. At one of his first IEP meetings, a school psychologist who had "interviewed" Isaac was giving the report and said, "Isaac told me that he lives in Beardstown with his parents, Mike and Denise."

Well, no, not really. Perhaps a classmate of his does, and apparently, Isaac learned that info and just repeated it. I think he gives unreliable answers when he just doesn't feel like talking or to be silly. He just says something to get the person to move on. He also tends to agree with whatever you suggest just to be accommodating.

"Hey, Isaac, want to go outside?"

"Yes."

"Hey, Isaac, want to stay inside?"

"Yes."

Aunt Sally Stock says she can tell when he's saying something just to accommodate because he sort of tilts his chin down and apologetically says yes. But then there are times when Isaac's words are right on!

One Sunday when eating lunch, he kept saying "cow."

SOMETHING EXTRA

"Yes, Isaac, we have cows." Then I looked up and saw that there was a cow in our driveway! Ah, yes, cow shouldn't be there!

And when he matter-of-factly said, "Tree falling down" when he was watching a storm out the window. Yep, a large branch was falling down!

Or when his dad had fallen on the ice and been rendered unconscious this past winter. "Isaac, where's your dad?"

"Fell."

He's a funny guy to talk to. He likes to get a good laugh from you. So if his talk is far-fetched and silly, he's having a great time with you, and you're making his day!

81

I've tried to post positive experiences about Isaac, but I don't want folks to get the impression that things are always glorious and full of rainbows with Isaac around. Having Isaac has been a bittersweet blessing at times.

Like other parents, my mind sometimes drifts to the things my son is incapable of achieving, the relationships he is missing out on, the experiences he won't be able to have, the "what if" questions. I feel like he is happy and content with his life. Does he know any different? Does he realize he's "missing out" on things in life that typical people enjoy? Is the quality of life he's living now good enough for him? Does he understand that he's hit a plateau in development and this is "as good as it gets"? Does that even matter?

The worries of a parent of a child with a disability differ from typical parental worries, not necessarily "worse" worries, just different. There are some worries I don't/won't have with Isaac that I have with my typical kids. Parents of typical kids can expect their children to grow up and become self-sufficient and have a life of their own. Isaac is not at a level of intelligibility/skill where I can ever expect that. He will always need self-help care and supervision.

It's tough to find a "babysitter" for a sixteen-year-old, and I'll be searching for sitters for him his whole life! There's also a spiritual side of it which I lie awake at night struggling with I can teach and foster religious faith in my typical kids. Is Isaac's understanding of God and faith enough? How can I help him have faith in God so that he will be able to enjoy eternal life one day? Will he be scared when it is his time to die? Will he know what's happening? How would I ever begin to prepare him for something he doesn't understand? Does he know what faith is? Is he capable of understanding it?

SOMETHING EXTRA

In my typical kids, I can start it and give them as much foundation as possible, but then the responsibility to continue their faith is ultimately theirs. It will always be my responsibility with Isaac. I try to limit the amount of time my mind travels to "what if," but I'm human, and I find myself there occasionally.

Isaac, singing his heart out during an elementary Christmas program

82

My goal is always to help people understand Isaac better, learn a little about Down syndrome, and give a glimpse into our daily life! For those who read them, thanks for taking the time to learn about Isaac and Down syndrome. My goals were to help people understand him better, learn a little about Down syndrome, and give a glimpse of our daily life. I also want you to feel free to ask me questions about Isaac or Down syndrome. If there's something you're curious about, talk to me, send me a message, just ask! I have appreciated all of your positive remarks and compliments. But I do want to quash one more "myth."

I don't subscribe to the belief that God gives special children to special parents or that I am in any way a special parent. Many children are born into loving and responsible homes, but there are plenty of kids with/without special needs born into pretty bad situations. God picked me to be Isaac's mom, just like He picked me to be the mom of Lydia and Charlie and the stepmom to Aaron. It just so happens that Isaac has an extra twenty-first chromosome in every cell of his body. And I do what I feel any responsible parent would do for their child, whether that child is born with ADD, diabetes, mental illness, eating disorder, or any special circumstance.

As parents, we should advocate and go the proverbial extra mile for our kids no matter the situation. I'm only doing what parents do every day, and it makes me no more special than any other parents. You'd do the same and you ARE doing the same for your children. Don't give me the glory. Give the glory to God for creating individuals who can teach us about the simple things in life, who can make us appreciate every day, who can show us happiness we didn't know existed, who are uninhibited and "raw." It was God's plan that I have

SOMETHING EXTRA

Isaac. There are days it is an overwhelming struggle, but it is an overwhelming privilege and joy to be given this responsibility to care for and be a witness to the life of Isaac Timothy French!

About the Author

Jill Roegge is the mom of Isaac, who was born with Down syndrome twenty years ago. She is also a mom to Lydia (twenty-six), Charlie (eight), and stepmom to Aaron (thirty-four). Jill and her husband, Matthew, live on a farm in a well-blended family, where she attempts to act as ringmaster of her little circus.

After growing up in a small, rural central Illinois community, Jill graduated from Illinois College with a degree in music. She plays the organ for her church and is the office manager for a small family business. Jill is on the board of directors for the local Special Olympics committee, where she has coached teams as well as assisted in the operation of the local basketball tournament.

CPSIA information can be obtained
at www.ICGtesting.com
Printed in the USA
LVHW010421210819
628264LV00011B/225/P